Adva

KristaLyn's bright, shining heart shows through in every word of this book as she gives writers a clear, positive path toward reaching self-awareness before they even begin the writing process. I can't imagine a better guide for healing – and I'm talking about both the book and the author. Two very enthusiastic thumbs up.

— Carrie White-Parrish, Editorial Director
Glass House Press/Eleven&Co/Spitfire Press

Driven Fearless

DRIVEN
FEARLESS

The Complete Roadmap to
Facing Your Fears and *Driving Forward*

KristaLyn A. Vetovich

NEW YORK

LONDON • NASHVILLE • MELBOURNE • VANCOUVER

Driven Fearless

The Complete Roadmap to Facing Your Fears and Driving Forward

Published in New York, New York, by Morgan James Publishing in partnership with Difference Press. Morgan James is a trademark of Morgan James, LLC.
www.MorganJamesPublishing.com

ISBN 9781642798166 paperback
ISBN 9781642798173 eBook
Library of Congress Control Number: 2019950066

Cover and Interior Design by:
Chris Treccani
www.3dogcreative.net

Morgan James is a proud partner of Habitat for Humanity Peninsula and Greater Williamsburg. Partners in building since 2006.

Get involved today! Visit
MorganJamesPublishing.com/giving-back

To my husband and parents, thank you for smiling and nodding when I don't make sense and for laughing at my rants. Looks like we finally made it!

Table of Contents

Introduction

ife is an incredible journey, but let's be honest, sometimes it feels like a complete wreck. You expect it to be the red convertible, thick sunglasses, flowing scarf, Pinterest-perfect road trip, but real life has potholes. Real life has other drivers who aren't watching the road. In real life, sometimes you get lost and there's no GPS to passive-aggressively recalculate your route. It's enough to stop you from getting behind the wheel at all.

What happened in your life that took you from driven to done?

With *Driven Fearless*, I will not only give you daily routines to manage your fears and anxiety, but also to reduce fear and panic altogether. I won't tell you you're weak for being afraid. You can be afraid of butterflies and still have a perfectly good reason for it. I want you to see you're strong enough to be whatever you choose to be, and that you have the power to choose to be fearless.

In this book you'll learn how to prevent a panic attack, how to catch fear and stop it before it grips you, and how to manage anxiety even if it catches you off guard.

Whatever your fears, one thing is for sure, they aren't meant to be in the driver's seat. It's time to kick your fears to the curb and take your life back into your own hands.

This isn't just a roadmap for people who experience travel anxiety. It can work for anyone who is ready for a practical approach to overcoming their fears. In this book, I'm going to ride shotgun with you and help you navigate your life your way. I'll be your GPS, copilot, and supportive friend to help take you beyond whatever caused your fear so you can live your passion and purpose with the simple, applicable steps that will take you beyond just driven. You'll be *Driven Fearless*.

Chapter One:

What the Accident Really Took from You

"I could have fed a lion," my mother lamented to me.

That phrase has become a running joke in my family, but those were the first words that sprang to my mother's mind after a Bulgarian challenged her with a bottle of local moonshine – and she won.

Her message didn't sink in for me that night. I was fourteen and too concerned that she must have received

1

dire news from her doctor or even from my doctor for her to act this overcome with regret – until dad explained to me that this was what being drunk looked like.

But five years later, those were the words echoing in my head as I jumped into the Nile River, took the reins of my life into my own hands, and told anxiety to take the back seat from then on (Pro Tip: Don't jump into the Nile River. It's not safe, but no one told me that. At least I'll always have that memory).

What would you rather have: the anxiety or the freedom to get out there to create memories? Since you're reading this book, I think we both know the answer.

You know what you want. That's not why you're here. You're looking for the steps you need to take your life back into your own hands and see results. I hear you.

What You Don't Need

You had a traumatic experience, and I'll bet plenty of people have offered you canned advice like, "Time will heal all wounds," "It's just something you have to live with," or my personal favorite, "Just get over it," but if you could just get over it, then you would be able to drive anywhere you wanted to by now. You'd be feeding the proverbial lion rather than standing by and watching as someone else takes the opportunity.

Do they think you chose to be forced out of your own car by random spells of pure, unadulterated terror?

Of course you didn't, but that's what happens when you try to drive ever since the accident, and all you want is someone to give you some real, practical, applicable advice that finally works.

Yes, time helps give perspective, but you've given yourself that. We only get so much time in life, and the last thing you want is to spend it panicking when you could be enjoying yourself instead. It should be that simple, but for some reason, it isn't!

You'd love to get over it. Before the accident, you had no problem with the family drives to the beach in the summer, or the commute to work, or just going to the grocery store in the car. Your vacation memories weren't riddled with anxiety and overridden by how horrible it was just to get from point A to point B. The accident happened to you, you didn't choose it.

Now you're stuck at home most days because just thinking about having to drive somewhere doesn't seem worth the destination. It's not that you think you're going to crash again like everyone seems to assume. It's just that being in the car triggers a panic attack which drains you and doesn't exactly leave you in a sociable mood. You may not know what it is about driving that triggers your anxiety. It just happens and it could happen at any time, so why take the chance and set yourself up for disappointment?

So you cancel girls' night, skip dates, wait until the movies come to Netflix, and spend your evening scrolling through social media filled with pictures of everyone else "living their best lives."

You know *why* you have anxiety. You were in a terrifying car accident. Your real question is how to stop it, and no one seems to know how to help you there. So it must not be so easy after all, huh?

You're ready to take your life back. You want to stop the panic attacks in the car and everywhere else they've crept into your life, to get out there and have a fancy date night, see the latest blockbuster in theaters, go to the beach and relax from the moment you leave the driveway to the moment you walk back through the door at the end of a luxuriously sunny week. But nothing you've tried so far has worked.

Just living with it isn't a solution. That's not enough. What you want are answers and that's what you've searched for.

You've read articles online, but they all say the same thing without actually saying anything helpful at all or telling you why they believe their techniques will work for you.

When you think about asking someone for help, it feels like they will all say the same thing: I don't know. That just makes you feel like a burden to them in the first place. On top of that, you hate that your friends are having fun without you and your husband just missed the third action movie release in a row because he's such a sweetheart, he won't go to the movies without you.

So you're stuck living with it, hoping time finally pulls through for you, and doing your best to just get over it… but is this really the life you're stuck with from now on?

What You *Do* Need

The answer, mercifully, is no. You do not have to live like this anymore, and you've picked up the last book you'll have to read on the subject.

Once you apply the techniques and ideas in this book, you will be able to get in the car and drive without a second thought. You'll be the envy of your friends' newsfeeds, the belle of the beach, and popcorn will be back on your menu again.

Wherever it is you want to go, you'll get there and you'll do it while breathing like a normal human being instead of having your body convince you you're about to die – which you aren't.

No more missed opportunities, no more memories that never got made. No more white knuckling the steering wheel with the radio off and nothing but the sound of your own heartbeat in your ears.

Take it from someone who's been there, there is so much more to conquering anxiety than simply breathing through it and waiting for it to strike again. You *can* manage your anxiety, but why stop there? What would your life look like if you could prevent panic attacks from happening in the first place?

You won't be that old woman who hits eighty-years-old with nothing to show for it. You won't be telling your daughter you *could* have fed a lion. You'll tell the story of how you did all the things you had the opportunity to do, and it starts today, with this book, these steps, and your God-given ability to do anything you set your mind to achieve.

Chapter Two:

Panic Doesn't Play Fair. Why Should You?

When I was little, as far back as my earliest memories, I used to hate bedtime. I didn't hate it for the same reason most kids do. It wasn't that I wanted to stay up and play. I just couldn't stand the panic that happened every single night as soon as I closed my eyes.

My parents would put me to bed and I'd beg them to stay with me until I fell asleep. They tried. They really did. I was read countless stories, had tons of theoretical conversations that only four-year-olds think of, and mom and I even made up our own language, but it took me forever to actually fall asleep. So eventually they'd kiss me goodnight and close the door. That's when it always happened. I'd close my eyes, start to drift to sleep, and out of nowhere just think about dying.

I don't know how I even figured out what dying was, but I knew for sure that it was the worst thing that could ever happen, and that death was out to take everything away from me.

The thoughts would creep into my mind slowly at first. Just a subtle reminder of my mortality, but one that wouldn't go away. Then it would go from a casual thought into, "It's going to happen. One day you're going to be a moment away from dying and there's nothing you can do to stop it."

That's about the point where I'd freak out, bolt from my bedroom, tear down the stairs, and throw myself into my parents' laps sobbing about not wanting to die.

Eventually, they'd settle me down and I'd be exhausted enough to fall asleep, but I never found anything that made it stop.

I had anxiety attacks nearly every night of my entire life until I was twenty-six years old, and not just before bed. As I grew up, the weird thoughts found equally weird places to pop up: when the lights went down at the movie theater, driving in the car, especially on long drives, even staring at the stars was terrifying. Just how far away they were made me feel small. And feeling small made me think of dying, which led to panic attacks.

I got better at holding the anxiety in after a while, but there would still be the doozies that would send me jumping up from the bed and hyperventilating, asking God to please help me.

When I was ten, I was diagnosed with a rare, incurable neurological disease called Moyamoya that required urgent surgery. I remember my mom saying, "Now you won't have to be afraid of dying anymore." Two things crossed my mind in that moment. One was I hadn't known about the disease when the fear started, and two that my fear was still noticeable to my family.

For the record, the surgery went great. It did what it was supposed to do and I was told to continue living my life normally.

Normal, for me, however, was still a life with panic attacks.

Even when I got engaged at twenty-three years old, I'd end up having a panic attack and waking my fiancé up with crazy fears about not wanting to get old because then I'd have to die. He did his best to help me through them, but as we continued to live together, got married, and moved into our new house, the anxiety was still there. It had even spread to making me think I was going to die every time my husband and I took a drive that lasted more than an hour. I felt trapped, like I'd never actually reach my destination and that there was no way I could survive this.

All I really had to do was sit down and read a book or something, but my mind would not allow that. Rationally, I knew everything was fine, but no one could convince my anxiety of that. I'm sure you understand the feeling.

It wasn't until a few months after moving into our first house with my then-husband that I finally decided my whole life was controlled by panic attacks and I wasn't going to allow that anymore.

Yes, death is a thing, but I don't want to hit eighty and look back on a life riddled with fear. I want to look back and have no regrets. If I can't enjoy now, I'm wasting all the time I do have. It wasn't a new concept to me, but until this moment the idea felt like a useless cliché. Now, it made sense because I came to the realization in my own way, through my own process. So I was finally ready to do something about it.

I found a way to ignore the people who said I'd just have to live with it. Too many people had told me that for too many reasons, and I don't like hearing someone tell me I can't do something. I'm a challenge-motivated person, and I decided to prove to everyone, but mostly to myself, that I don't have to adjust the rest of my life around my anxiety. I can deal with it and run my life the way I want to run it.

I was already certified in various energy therapies, life coaching, spiritual coaching, and even nutritional coaching, so if I wasn't prepared to find the one solution to rule them all, I didn't know who was.

It only took me a few months before I figured out that anxiety is a power struggle. It's all about feeling in control. Why was I so afraid of dying? Because I couldn't stop it from happening. Why did a long car ride feel like being buried alive? Because I wasn't the one in control of the car and the amount of time spent on the journey. Time and not having enough of it was another huge fear of mine because I can't control time, only what I do with it.

What about driving makes you feel out of control? Is it the other drivers, traffic, your own instincts?

I combined all my experience and read a few new books until I found a way to show my anxiety who's boss, with tangible tools that I can actually use and a mindset to train my brain not to panic anymore, even when something unexpected triggers an attack.

Here's what you need to know:

1. Your anxiety isn't your fault, but it is a valid problem.

2. You may never really understand why driving gives you anxiety, but you can learn how to stop it anyway.

3. Driving without a panic attack will take some effort, but it won't take nearly as long as you've been dealing with it already, and it's definitely worth your time to try.

Once you understand what is in your control and what isn't in your control, then you'll be able to take the steps you need to conquer your anxiety and drive wherever and whenever you want, which I will outline for you in detail in the next chapter.

Chapter Three:

The Trick to Getting There and Back Again Safely

What is anxiety anyway? It's your body's way of handling stress. Makes sense right? You get scared, and your body releases the cortisol hormones it thinks you need in order to hightail it out of the situation and back to safety. But what happens when there's nowhere to run? What happens when you're stuck in the car until you get to your destination and you can't let all that extra energy out?

Like all suppressed emotions, it backs up and it can take roughly half an hour for the cortisol levels in your body to get back to normal. It's a chemical reaction, so it has to run its course, kind of like alcohol.

That just doesn't seem fair. How are you supposed to overcome something that seems like such an involuntary reaction? Most of the time, you hear that the solution is to treat a problem at its source, but you're not afraid of driving! You just panic when you're in the car, and the only explanation must be that somehow you're afraid of something having to do with driving, but as I explained in the last chapter, the car may not have anything to do with it. It could be something else entirely. So how, when you aren't sure of the source, do you manage your body's random fear triggers?

There's a trick to getting your feelings back under your control, and there's a way you can teach yourself not to let it happen again. You do it by giving your body a new definition of safety. You do it by literally retraining your brain to stop thinking that you're going to die every time you get in the car.

The trick isn't in the *how* as much as it's in understanding the *why*. I'm going to show you a new way to approach managing and preventing panic attacks. I'll also explain why all of it works because, while you've already heard or read plenty of opinions on how to adjust to anxiety, you may be as frustrated as I was to realize these supposedly life-changing secrets didn't give you a good enough reason to believe they would work for you. Otherwise, you wouldn't be here. Those methods would have satisfied you, and you wouldn't still be searching for answers.

It's important when doing anything new to have a reason to do it. When I was a fitness coach, the biggest thing we focused on, and the tool I've carried into all levels of my coaching today, is *why* are you doing this? What's it worth to you, and why is this specific method the best one to get you there? Feel free to think about it and write your answer here. Let it be the first thing that pops in your head. Why do you need to be able to drive again without anxiety? Why do you need to be the girl who can get behind the wheel again?

The Driven Fearless Road Map

We're going to take a trip together, a journey through this book. Every good trip has certain checkpoints that we'll cover in each chapter of what we'll call the Driven Fearless Road Map, with built-in rest stops for you to be able to check in with yourself and practice the steps to make sure they make sense for you personally. At the end of each chapter, you'll find exercises where you can follow the exercise and apply each step to your own life. By the end of this book, the Driven Fearless Road Map will be your personal road map, and you will be the woman!

Before your anxiety has a chance to deter you from reading any further, let me promise you that this is going to be fun! It's going to set the standard for every trip you take from now on. You're going to get real tools that really work with real explanations from someone who actually used them to solve this problem.

First, you need to understand how to plan for your next drive: your first drive without a panic attack. It's import not only to know where you're going, but how you're going to get there. What do you need to bring with you? What conditions will you be driving in? All of these things are important to give you a sense of control and to help you catch your brain before it can detour you to Crazy Town.

Next, we're going to understand how to navigate the unexpected, and how that might make your brain want to freak out. You'll learn what to do about the things you can't see coming, and how to know what's ahead as much as possible. It's just like having an updated GPS that keeps you posted on traffic conditions or checking the weather before a vacation. Understanding what's around you will help you handle things in the moment even if the drive doesn't go exactly according to plan.

Then, we'll get into the real tricks of how to heal once you know the reality of the road. You'll be able to convince your brain that there's nothing to panic about. We'll cover this both physically and mentally so you, your brain, and your body can all agree that there's no reason to panic while driving. In fact, driving should be enjoyable!

That's when we'll dig deeper to really understand anxiety triggers and what to do when something sets your anxiety off for no recognizable reason. The good news is, panic isn't the answer. It's control, and you can control more than you think. Bonus: I'm going to tell you why wanting a sense of control *isn't* bad even though society tells us it is (what is up with that, anyway?).

If you're anything like me, you want tangible steps, and you're reading this book because you want someone to tell you practical, applicable answers. That's what I'm going to give you. I don't want to just tell you that you can get better and spout theory at you. I want you to understand why this is going to work, and then I'll give you all the tools and exercises you need to tailor the process to your lifestyle and make it work for good. Even when you're not feeling mentally up to the challenge of fighting anxiety, you'll have options to get you through any situation.

Are You Ready to Roll?

It's time to ignore the people who believe you just have to live with anxiety, or the ones who say you should just take a pill to fix your problems. There's a place for medicine, I will never argue that, but you already know that medicine isn't going to fix your anxiety, it only helps mask it. You want permanent solutions. You can be the fearless woman that you used to be – but a new and improved version of her, because this book won't just heal your anxiety, it's going to rock your world.

Go ahead and plan your next family vacation, schedule a date night, pre-order your movie tickets, call the girls and tell them the next round of mojitos is on you, because you're about to be unstoppable.

Rest Stop: What Is My Why?

In a journal, write your "Why" so you know why it's worth it for you to be able to drive without having a panic attack. Whenever you're struggling to keep going with this process, come back here and remember why this process of reclaiming your life and your joy is worth it. In the next chapter, I'm going to tell you why this is the best way to conquer your panic.

Chapter Four:

Ways to Plan the Perfect Drive

et's start with the obvious. What's the first thing you're going to do before you take any trip? Plan it, right?

Going to the grocery store? You've got your list (which you usually don't stick to), you've got your wallet, your keys – do you need to get gas while you're at it? You know all of these things before you leave the house. You're on top of it. The accident didn't change that.

So let's plan that next drive. The one you take without any panic attacks. The one that leads to freedom and deep, steady breathing all the way back home.

But you already do that, right? This isn't anything new and you've tried it before. Simply planning doesn't work because you're not the only one on the road. You have to deal with animals darting across the street, construction forcing you to an infuriating detour on an unknown back road, other weirdos out there who clearly don't know how to drive. That's how you got in an accident in the first place. So what haven't you already tried that changes that?

The answer is simple, a bit unconventional, but that's better than the conventional things you've tried that haven't worked, right? Stick with me. You're going to get results this time.

You planned, and that's great, but did you *create* the drive? What if you could see the drive as if it's already happened, and know how it went before you left your house? Would that change the way you feel about it?

That's exactly what I'm talking about. It sounds insane, but it's called manifesting, and you do it every day without realizing it. Heck, it may have been a factor in what really caused your accident, but that's only because you didn't realize your power back then. Now you do and here's how you can use it.

Whose Road Is It Anyway?

"We are magic.
we are moments.
we are dreams and
we are memories.
we are everything."
–R.M. DRAKE

You are a wizard and you create your own destiny.

Maybe that sounds like an unrealistic bunch of malarkey to you. I know it did to me the first time someone tried to get me to jump on the manifesting train, but I like real answers. So when faced with the theory that I create my own reality, I didn't take anyone's word for it. I pursued evidence for myself.

I mentioned before that you manifest every day without realizing it, and I'm not kidding. You just never called it manifesting before, and the word can sometimes give the wrong idea. Manifesting doesn't have to mean conjuring something out of thin air. It can be as simple as making a sandwich.

Picture this: It's 11a.m., not quite your usual lunchtime, but you had Pilates this morning so your stomach has other ideas of when you should be feeding it. You feel that telltale grumble and your brain thinks, "Hmm. I'm hungry. What do I want to eat?"

You've just begun manifesting. You are deciding what it is you want and creating an image in your mind of what that looks like, how it'll taste, how much you'll enjoy eating it, the chips you'll pour on the plate to go along with it.

That is what manifestors call "visualization," and if you've ever had a daydream, then you already know what that feels like!

That's what I'm saying; you're already a pro at this. We're just making you aware of it so you can use your powers for good.

So you picture the sandwich. What happens next? Because it certainly isn't in your hands yet, and here's where a lot of people get stuck when it comes to manifesting.

If you search manifesting on Pinterest, you'll get flowery images telling you all it takes is a dream, a vision, and letting go. Just like a fairytale. But there's something they don't tell you: You have to walk the path to get there.

Take our sandwich for example. Looks good in your head, but it'll be even better once it's on your plate where you can take the massive bite out of it you earned at Pilates this morning.

How do you get from "I want a sandwich" to "I have a sandwich?" You know the answer to this one, but bear with me as I guide you through the metaphor.

You get up and head to the kitchen. You gather everything you need for the sandwich. You don't grab anything you don't need, because why would you? That won't help the sandwich get to your plate any faster. You assemble the sandwich, pour the chips, grab a drink, and head to the couch to watch some HGTV, and you enjoy every moment of peace while the sandwich lasts.

That's real-life manifesting in all its glory.

If you want another example, think of trying to have a baby. You don't just wake up pregnant the day after you decide you want kids, do you? You decide if having a baby is something you're ready for, take the necessary – ahem – *course of action*, prepare the nursery, visit the doctor, pick names, throw parties, and imagine with all your heart how your life is going to be different once your son or daughter arrives. Then you make the lifestyle changes necessary to welcome this bundle of joy into your world.

Manifesting. Making it happen. Creating ahead of time.

Quantum physics also supports this theory, so there is science to it, but you don't need to hear about matter and photons and whatever. Let's sum it up in a quote from Walt Disney: "If you can dream it, you can do it." It turns out the biggest imaginations in history, people like Tesla and Disney, were masters of manifesting. They wanted something and made it real.

What you want to do is get to the grocery store without incident and maybe the beach later this summer with your family (by the way, planning a vacation? Manifesting). So let's talk turkey. In aisle six at the grocery store. Where you're going. In your car. Without a panic attack.

Because you *can* do this.

Visualize: The Drive Before the Drive

The first step in manifesting is knowing what you want, right? Try that right now. What do you want? It could be a safe and efficient drive, it could be arriving at the destination, it could be the turkey in aisle six. What motivates you to decide to really do this the most? It could be the same Why you wrote back in chapter three, but if you can think of more reasons, even better! Add them to your list!

Now picture what you want the way you would picture a sandwich. What does it feel like to get in the car and drive confidently and without anxiety? Do you listen to music? Do you check your mirrors without your palms sweating on the wheel? Are you wearing sunglasses because that's your style, or is it too cloudy for that?

Follow yourself along the road to wherever you're going in this scenario. There are other cars, maybe some construction, or a squirrel with a death wish, those things aren't in your control (but, don't worry, I'll cover how to handle that in chapter five).

What do you do if you encounter any of these things? What does the fearless woman who successfully arrived at her destination do when the unexpected pops up? You know this because that person looks, acts, and thinks exactly as you do. She just doesn't have panic attacks anymore because she conquered them.

Do you swerve but regain control? Do you hit the brakes, puff your cheeks, and keep on driving?

Let's say someone does rear-end you – God forbid – what would the fearless woman do then? You can't control the other driver, but you *can* control your reaction and you can know what that reaction looks like right now. It's the same as taking a CPR class even though you may never need to use it, or running any emergency plan.

Consider this your fire drill. Remember those in school? The drill bell went off and you didn't even think. You stood up, got in line, and took the predetermined course safely out of the school.

What is that predetermined course for you? Tip your head back against the couch, close your eyes, and plan your route knowing that this is what will happen. This is how you, the girl behind the wheel, handle situations, whatever they are.

Making Space: Only Bring What You Need

There's no room for anxiety if you already have a solution to fill its space.

That's the most tangible, important, practical mindset when it comes to manifesting. When I was trying to understand how manifesting really works, this was the piece that made it all click.

Make space for what you want to manifest in your life and only that. If there is something in your life that is allowing space for anxiety, replace it. Throw it out just as you would anything in the fridge that you don't want to eat. Your anxiety is expired. You don't need it anymore and it doesn't serve you. It's taking up space and starting to smell weird. Trash it.

Think about the family preparing for a baby. Maybe you have kids, maybe you don't, or maybe your animals are your children. Either way, you've seen new parents go through this. They find out they're pregnant and suddenly, there's a whole other person that has to share space in their house. So what do they do about that? Do they shrug and leave things the way they are? In a majority of cases, no. They clear out an entire room to make space for this new little life that they're excited to welcome into their home. So imagine the things in your head right now. Your body is where your soul lives. If you've got a big heart, and I know you do, is it getting a little crowded in there with anxiety taking up all that space and all your attention? Are your thoughts, the things that create your very reality, distracted by fear to the point that they can't even entertain nice things?

If your heart is your mother and your soul is your father, let's call your brain the nursery. How can you make space in the nursery for a healthy, happy mind? You have to clear out the clutter.

If that sounds impossible to you, don't worry. I'm not going to judge you, and frankly, no one has the right to. This is your process. If you can't fathom the whole manifesting thing, fake it until it makes more sense. You've been putting on the "act" that you're okay when you're not for a while now. The difference here is that now you know it isn't an act, it's the version of yourself that you are creating. So next time you "fake it," own it. Don't doubt yourself. Don't judge yourself for being a fraud. Stand tall and be that person who is okay – really okay. She's who you deserve in your life. She's who you already are. Let her out.

And when you've gotten the hang of visualizing and making space, there's good and there's bad news.

Take Action: Pack Your Things

The good news is, you now have the motivation you needed to take the actual steps to make your vision come true, the same way you are motivated by the sandwich to walk to the kitchen. You know what the safe and efficient trip looks like, and you know everything that goes along with it. So you know how to make it all happen. You know how to act when the unexpected occurs. You may take a less busy route because it feels safer for you. You want to get in the car because you already know it's going to be better than okay.

Fun Fact for people who grew up in the church like me: praying without ceasing, that thing they always said was the best thing you could do, in my opinion, is manifesting.

What if you thought of your feelings as prayers or as intentions? What if the thoughts that come from those feelings become your visualizations, prayers to God to send you what is on your mind? Are you asking for a successful and efficient drive? The evidence suggests not. That's why you've had panic attacks up until now.

I'll talk more about what to do with this newfound knowledge and how to follow the most challenging step of manifesting – releasing – in the following chapters, but now you know, and that's all you need to make the world a better place, to be your own hero.

I bet if you pictured the hero you need, she'd look a lot like the girl in your visualization. That's because you already are your own hero. You are the fearless woman. You just didn't realize it until now.

Rest Stop: Visualize & Make Space

Here's how I want you to move forward before you even look at the next chapter. If you didn't visualize your next trip, the one where you don't panic at all, do it now and write it down in your journal. Better yet, open up Pinterest and create a vision board. That's what Pinterest is, after all – one vast vision board. You've already visualized your closet and the food you want to make and the way you want to design your bathroom, so why not this? Pin an image of your destination. Pin an image of the dolled up Marilyn Monroe driving a '57 Chevy, wind tossing her hair and that scarf that I'm not sure really does anything while she clutches her sun hat to her head, even though she's already wearing big sunglasses.

You know the kind of picture I mean.

Pin the things you're going to do at the destination. Keep the questions below in mind. Are you driving alone or is this a girls' road trip? It can be anything you want it to be! Make it yours because that's what this life is!

You are at the wheel. Anxiety and fear aren't even in the back seat. Lock those jerks in the trunk and blast the radio so you can't hear their screams. You've got places to be, things to do, memories to make, even if they're small.

And if you're still worried about those other issues of the road, the ones you can't control like weather conditions and bad drivers who don't use their headlights when it rains, keep reading. You've only just begun, and I'm not going to pull a Mary Poppins on you and disappear any time soon.

Reality is only what you make it. That's an actual fact, and that's manifesting. So if this is the life you're creating with God/Universe/Source (who/which controls all the stuff you don't) are you happy with it? Again, you bought this book, so I'd wager you're looking for a change, and if it's positive, safe, change you want, you can have it right now.

My Next Trip Journal Questions:

1. Where am I going?

2. How do I handle the unexpected?

3. Who is with me?

4. What am I most excited about?

5. My driving playlist:

Chapter Five:

How to Prepare for the Unexpected

So you get that there are some things you can control and some things you can't. Everyone has free will to make their own choices with unique outcomes and consequences, and sometimes it all crashes together – literally. That's life, right? But is that everything there is to it?

When I was growing up, grown-ups always told me I had to be patient because God's timing isn't the same as mine. Naturally, my response was, "Well, then God should hurry up or at least tell me what's taking Him so long."

If you had this grievance too, I'm betting you also heard the classic response: "Well, to God, a minute could be a thousand years. After all, Jesus said he'd return 'soon' two thousand years ago."

Let's discuss how well *that* went over in the mind of the girl who panicked about death and dying every night. To me, divine timing was the dumbest thing in the world, and God must have been lazy if it took Him so long to do everything. Maybe God had all the time in the world, but I, a mere mortal, did not.

That grudge stuck with me, and I think God did it on purpose, because I've spent most of my life tipping my face toward the sky and asking for signs to help me understand how to work with His timing rather than against it, if only to get people to stop calling me impatient for once.

Guess what? I believe I found the secret. And I'm not good at keeping secrets, so I'm more than happy to spill the beans to you right here and right now.

I found divine timing exactly where I was looking for it: in the sky.

Your Cosmic Weather Map: Astrology

Have you ever browsed Facebook and seen those memes blaming Mercury retrograde for everything? How can you blame a planet for life being rough? Technically, you can't. I'm not going to throw you for that big of a loop...

However, I am going to suggest that God's divine timing is in the stars. Don't worry, I'll tell you exactly how I got there and why I came to believe that astrology is not against God, but rather *by* Him *for* us.

When I first felt a tug of interest toward astrology, I ignored it for years. Astrology was bad news. It was idolatry or something that would lead me down a dangerous path, but still, the signs and hints that I should investigate it popped up all around me. It was always in the corner of my mind, so I asked that, if I was meant to pursue astrology, could God please make that unquestionably clear to me.

One day, my dad brought home a DVD about the Star of Bethlehem. It sounded interesting, so I watched it with him and my world exploded. The DVD was the permission I had asked for to start exploring astrology on a deeper level. I now believe it was a calling to do it.

In case you have similar inhibitions about astrology, let me illustrate why I believe that God uses the stars to speak to us.

In the beginning, God created the stars "for signs, and for seasons, and for days, and years," (Gen. 1:14-15 (KJV)) and I think we all can agree He did a wonderful job, but why have we been so caught up in them ever since? Why were the stars used to draw the wise men to the Nativity? Why were they the promise given to Abraham about his innumerable children? Why do we name them and use them to guide our ships and bring meaning to our lives? Where did that yearning for a connection, that awe, come from? We even gave them the highest honor of being the location of Heaven and God's place of residence, however we imagine that works.

These days, it's easier to understand Heaven as another vibration of being, but that's a whole other book that I'd love to share with you someday. For now, let's stay here on Earth and simply look up.

What do you see when you look up (and please don't stare at the sun. You know what I'm getting at here)? You see the sky, the stars, the darkness between, or the blue all around.

I see a clock. I see intention. I see something I can use to plan my life in line with all those things I can't control. I see the way to control the uncontrollable, not in an arrogant way, but in a co-creative way.

God Is Your Travel Agent: Co-Creation

When I first learned the ThetaHealing® Technique, the books and then my instructor explained prayers and intentions in a new way. The creator of the ThetaHealing® Technique, Vianna Stibal, claimed that we don't need to ask God for things, but that we can command *with* God to co-create our realities, blending His divine timing with our intentions to bring things, situations, anything into being. She even offers the definition of "command" as something done literally "with God" in comparison to "demand." I'm not saying you should stomp your foot and demand God give you a safe an anxiety-free drive. That would be your ego talking anyway.

What I am saying is it is totally acceptable for you to take your place as the "co" in command and work with God to bring the safe drive into your reality.

You already know how to do your part. It's called manifesting, and we talked about how that works in chapter four. The missing part of the equation is God and what He's up to behind the scenes.

That would be divine timing, but you can know that too. And, sure, you can't change it, but you can use tools such as astrology, treat it like you would a weather report, and plan your trip accordingly.

Check the Forecast: Your Cosmic Weather Report

If you're like me, every morning you stroll through your house and call out, "Hey, Google. What's the weather today?" to understand how warm you should dress and what type of shoes you should wear. If Google says it's going to rain, you don't wear your silk flats. You bring your rain boots and pull your weatherproof coat out of the closet.

You already co-create with Google and your weatherman. Why not with God?

It all begins with your astrology birth chart. That's your energetic comfort zone – the cosmic climate you were born in. Every change after that moment is going to feel easy, hard, or somewhere in between depending on how it reacts with your comfort zone. These are called transits: the current position of the planets and how they affect your birth placements.

Don't worry, I'm not going to dump all the astro-jargon on you here, even though it's really cool and fascinating. You now know all the terms you need to get you through this book and the rest of your life as far as managing your anxiety is concerned.

If you look at your birth chart, which you can easily find online by searching "my astrology birth chart," you'll see your chart and you'll even get a computer-generated explanation of the chart. With this, you can find out pretty much everything you need to know about who you are, what you like, what you don't like, the list goes on. It doesn't quite compare to a real-life interpretation, but it'll serve your purpose. The really cool part is you can also get a feel for your divine timing from your chart. Yours specifically.

You can figure it out for the world in general too, but the world isn't the one trying to get back into the car and drive safely. You are, and that's what I care about.

So you see your life purpose on a chart of weird symbols that somehow reflects what the sky looked like three decades ago. How does that help you get to the beach without a car accident?

Remember: weather report. Let's roll with the beach analogy for a bit.

When you go to the beach and you're trying to decide which week of summer you want to go, what's the first thing you think of? I'm guessing you want to enjoy time in the sun, so you're not going to pick the week with rain in the forecast for five of the seven days you'll be there.

You're looking into the future, getting an idea of the conditions you can expect and planning accordingly. In this case, you choose the week that's expected to be sunny.

Astrology works the same way. You can look at your divine timing, your transits which you can also find generic interpretations for through a simple search, and figure out which week is best suited for you to be able to relax and enjoy. You can even narrow it down to which week – which specific day – is best, safest, and most comfortable for *your* travel!

This isn't a new concept. Remember, the Wise Men did it. Even more recently, Ronald Reagan was known to use astrology to help him perform well in his campaigns. Astrology is often consulted when people are establishing new businesses or even cities such as Baghdad. It's not in the mainstream right now, but that doesn't mean it isn't being used.

You can use your divine timing for everything, and it will not only help you plan your trips, but you can understand why things happen around you, realize if you're off track or if you're just going through a hard time – and if you are, you can find the purpose in it because the area of your birth chart will tell you exactly what in your world is going on and even for how long!

Astrology is proof that not only did God know the moment you would be born from the beginning of time, but also that you were *meant* to be born. You are here for a reason. Your existence is part of divine timing. You have a divine purpose that isn't finished yet, and even *who* you are is totally okay because you'll find it written all over the interpretation of your birth chart, which is like a massive stamp from God on your forehead that says 'Approved.' God made the world, He made time, and He made you. He absolutely has time for you. God's timing, as mentioned at the beginning of this chapter, can be whatever He wants it to be. So He can definitely make time especially for you. And He did. He mapped it out and put it in the stars back when everything was first created. Your birth chart is your proof that you are intentional, special, and most of all, safe.

Your Daily Outlook: Numerology

You can also combine astrology with other tools like numerology to narrow down your divine timing.

Numerology is easier to figure out because it's just simple addition. With numerology, you get exactly what it says on the tin: numbers. These numbers can be used to explain the type of year, month, day, even life you're having. The number that explains your life purpose is called your Ruling Number and you can find that by adding all the numbers of your birthday together until you get a single digit number like this:

12/12/1986: 1+2+1+2+1+9+8+6= 30

3+0= 3

The meaning of that number will give you an idea of what your soul came here to accomplish, which can be found with greater detail with astrology as well. Don't worry, I've got a free cheat sheet to help you work all this out and understand what it means at the end of the chapter. Numbers were never really my thing, and I won't abandon you to them either.

You can also figure out your Personal Year Number, which lets you know what kind of year it's going to be for you. There's a way to do this in astrology as well, but for numerology, you just do the same thing you did before, except using the current year instead of your birth year. The number you get will tell you the theme of this year for you.

From there, you can even blend the month and day numbers in to get a full-figured picture of the energy that day holds for you personally. Mix that with your transits and you'll wonder why anyone was ever confused about God's timing in the first place! You can download a free cheat sheet at the end of this book to help explain what the numbers mean for you and how to use them, and I've added a brief version of it to the Rest Stop journal exercise at the end of this chapter.

You can't control divine timing, but you can understand it and work with it. Co-creation. Using this co-creative forecast will help you decide how to tackle each day, which I'll lay out for you in a satisfyingly organized journal page in chapter ten.

Until then, let's not forget your built-in divine timing radar: your feelings. Your feelings create your thoughts, which create your reality like we talked about in chapter four. They also can help you understand more about your divine timing moment by moment.

Trust Your Gut

Let's say astrology and numerology are great, but you forget to check them some days when life gets crazy. That's cool, because you've got your own meter for when things are good and when they aren't. It's called your gut instinct, and it carries you moment by moment through every single day. It was with you the day you had your accident, and it's probably feeling a bit neglected since then with those panic attacks taking up all your attention.

I believe your gut, intuition, instincts, conscience, whatever you prefer to call it is how your higher self – the part of you that understands your divine timing – talks to you. It's the part of you that is part of God (the Holy Spirit part of the Trinity, if you like). That's why it does weird, seemingly impossible things like warning you something is bad before you have proof that it is, or giving you the creeps about someone who turns out to be untrustworthy.

Trust your gut. As you get in the car, when you sit behind the wheel and think about how your drive is going to happen, see what your gut says. Ignore the panic, that's just your brain trying to keep you safe. Thank it, but assure it that you're just fine, and focus on what's truly real. Picture the drive. How do you feel? Good? Bad? Nothing?

Nothing doesn't mean you're doing it wrong. Nothing means you're in the moment and God is asking you to trust Him. I'd rather feel nothing than bad any day. Nothing is a success and you should praise yourself for it.

Navigate a Rainy Day: What to Do When Time Isn't on Your Side

But what if whatever is coming on this trip is bad, and your gut is keeping secrets from you?

This is when you get to do something freakishly cool. You get to talk to your higher self. Now, you might think your higher self is some tall, all-knowing, spirit thing, but I've found that when I look to my higher self and the higher selves of others, I often find myself face-to-face with a little kid.

That's not a bad thing. Kids are brilliant. They still believe in magic, and honestly, they're right to. Manifesting is magic, praying is magic. Co-creating *with* God is magic, so why do we stop believing?

Scientifically, it's because of brain waves. Children from the ages of one to seven primarily use what's called the theta brain wave. This is the same brain wave that's used in the ThetaHealing® Technique and in hypnotism, and that's because it's the brain wave that stored our subconscious beliefs while we were kids. Once you get older, you shift into the alpha and beta brain waves you're used to today, and things can start to feel a little less magical. Your gut instincts, however, can help you remember what magic feels like, and they will guide you through your everyday divine timing.

When you get a bad feeling, you might be tempted to react out of fear and retreat, but don't. Take a pause, go somewhere quiet, close your eyes, picture that inner/higher self the way you would a lost child and ask her what's going on. What can you do to help? If you see an adult when you close your eyes, then ask what you need to know. It's the same concept. You're still doing it right.

You'll get a feeling or a phrase or an image in response, and it'll probably surprise you to find that it isn't an image of another car accident at all. It's something you forgot in the house or something you need to remember to do or someone that you need to call and check on. It could even be a fear left over from when you were seven that you just haven't fixed yet. We'll talk more about how to handle those in chapter ten.

Check Your Signals: The Signs Around You

You'll start to notice that your feelings, astrological transits, the numerology of the day in the context of your Personal Year Number, and all those things are falling into alignment around you. They're whispering to you, giving you your morning energy report and suggesting how you can make the most of this day by planning accordingly.

When you want to plan a trip or take a drive anywhere, check the energetic weather. Most of the time, it's going to be a good day to drive. Very rarely it may not be, but at least you know what to look for so you can plan around it. You can live your entire life aligned with that divine timing, which will do more to help you avoid the accidents than anything else will. Because I've got a secret for you. That accident wasn't an accident. It happened for a reason. In a way, you needed it, so the Universe delivered.

Divine timing isn't evil. You might also argue that it's not necessarily good either. It's more neutral and colored by your manifesting and choices. Divine timing is unconditional love, which is the essence of God. It doesn't change. It's a constant. Like vanilla ice cream. You are always loved and God always wants what's best for you, but when you love someone you let them go in the hopes they'll choose to come back to you. You're the one with free will. The toppings on the ice cream sundae. You get to choose which roads you take, even if that means a detour from your divine timing, and God allows it because it's the flavor of life you want.

Recalculating When You Take a Wrong Turn

I bet you just had a mini panic attack, worrying that you've abandoned God, ruined your entire life, and missed your purpose or something. Calm down. You can't mess up that badly. This is exactly what divine timing is for.

Sometimes you might be off track and divine timing – God – will do what it takes to help you get back. He'll give you a nudge, but you may not notice it. Then He'll call out to you, but so much is going on in your life that you just don't hear it over the noise, so He has to yell, then finally before you get too far away: Godsmack. I like to call events like this "Godsmacks," because they're difficult things that happen to break our concentration so we can refocus on what's important. It isn't pleasant, but it gets your attention the same way a parent guides a child (we do call God "the Father," after all). God isn't out to get you when bad things happen. On the contrary, He's yanking you back before you stumble off the cliff you didn't see.

What you come to understand is the accident didn't happen to scare you and to debilitate you. Much like the bad feeling, it happened to get your attention. We'll talk about that more in chapter six, but here are the blunt facts: yes, you had an accident, but you didn't die. There's a reason behind that. It means you have more that you're meant to accomplish in this life, otherwise, you'd have passed away in the accident. So rather than allowing the anxiety to control you, why not be excited that you have an important purpose to fulfill and try to understand what the accident was trying to tell you instead? Once you know that, you won't need the anxiety anymore. It will go away. These days, whenever something goes wrong, I simply look up and ask, "What was that for? What do You want me to learn from this?"

You can be conscious of the meaning behind things that happen in your life. You can understand day by day, moment by moment, so you won't have to deal with a Godsmack like that again. If you understand divine timing, if you intentionally work along with it – co-create – you won't need accidents to bring you back on track. You won't get lost to begin with, and with that knowledge, when things do get tough, you'll know that it's just an experience to help you grow, not a punishment for being wrong or straying from your life path. You'll know every day what your purpose is, you'll reap the rewards of a life lived to the fullest, and every time you get in the car, God will be your passenger for a safe and efficient drive to anywhere you want to go.

Rest Stop: Find Your Divine Timing

Now that you understand what divine timing is and how it works around you, let's make it tangible.

This is the ultimate factor in your road map to healing, and everything that follows will add to it in a specific way that brings your life into clarity and control so you can avoid anxiety, not only in the car but all the time.

Use the bullet journal section below to practice understanding your divine timing.

Here are some things to keep in mind:

- What is the numerology day number (the date)?
- What is your Personal Year Number (the sum of your birthday this year)?
- Do any major astrological events affect you today that you should be aware of?

Numerology Cheat Sheet

How to simplify:
Date Example: 5/8/1990
5+8+1+9+9+0= 32
3+2= 5
General Interpretations:

#	Ruling Number	Personal Year Number
1	Self-Actualization	Rediscovering Self
2	Emotion	Deciding attachment/worth
3	Logic	Planning
4	Organizing	Structuring
5	Compassion	Sharing
6	Thinking outside the norm	Creative expansion
7	Sacrifice	Consolidating
8	Theory/Teaching	Accepting as theory
9	Ideology	Applying as ideology

Write any notes or interesting things that stand out to you in your journal so you can understand it in your own terms!

Chapter Six:

Secrets to Preventing and Managing Panic Attacks

So, now you understand the exterior forces at work when it comes to why your accident happened in the first place, and how to make sure it doesn't happen again, but just in case you're still feeling nervous about how horrible panic attacks feel and dreading it creeping up on you anyway, let's talk about what to do before and during a panic attack.

In chapter four, you learned how to visualize and prepare for a safe drive and anything that might go awry. So you've got that to work with, but I want you to feel like you are in control, which we'll delve into even more in chapter seven, because control isn't always a bad thing.

What steps can you take to help you feel better in the moment? What are your physical resources to heal your panic attacks?

How to Live in the Moment

Social media always shows us images of random people standing on mountaintops, arms flung wide as if hugging life itself, and tells us that's what "living in the moment" looks like. Let's get real for a minute here: social media is not reality. Social media sets expectations for unrealistic realities that aren't as fulfilling as they look. So the first step to understanding your resources to prevent and manage panic attacks is to realize that what you see on your news feed is not the whole picture. The people behind the smiles and cocktails have just as many problems as you do, sometimes more. They have struggles, but most of them aren't taking pictures of *that* with a #nofilter.

Social media is in and of itself a filter on our lives. And that's fun! There's nothing wrong with displaying what you're excited or proud of as long as you understand that the flip side of the coin and the moments that don't happen in front of the camera are not considered failure. They're life. They're learning. They're your process and you are definitely not the only one still trying to figure your life out.

Social media *can* be a great tool for learning how to live in the moment when used wisely. It gives you a literal snapshot of the moment, but it's what happens next that makes the difference: you caption it. You consciously write what that moment means for you, what happened, and how it affects your life. When used for joy and gratitude, social media is #blessed. But when it causes you to compare yourself to others, that is definitely not the moment you want to be living in. It's not the reality you want to create.

I believe there's a time for living in the moment, but that doesn't mean it's the only place to be.

Often, we find ourselves living in the past or dwelling on the future. That's great when we're reminiscing on happy memories or planning our dreams (*cough cough* manifesting), but it's not so great when we're panicking about the worst thing that could possibly happen when we get in the car, or when we're freaking out about how horrible the accident was when it happened. How are you supposed to find a balance?

Let's start here and now with living in the moment. What does that even mean? I remember a few weeks before my wedding, I was panicking. I didn't care about the details or the cake or anything like that. I intentionally kept the wedding simple so I wouldn't have anything to worry about, managing my anxiety even then. I had nothing to stress over leading up to my special day. No, I was panicking because everything was going right – *too right* – and I felt like I was surely going to lose something. Life couldn't possibly be this good without something going wrong (maybe you can relate?). I expressed this to my husband, and he took me by the shoulders, sadness in his eyes, and asked me to promise him something.

"Please do your best to be present in the moment on our wedding day," he said. "I don't want you to not remember it because you were too busy being out of the moment."

That hit me hard. My husband was worried I would mentally miss our wedding day. I realized I had a choice. I could continue the way I always had, which was seriously stressful, or I could figure out what living in the moment meant and start doing it.

Here's the good news: I remember every second of my wedding day. I did it. And so can you.

Fun Fact: in yoga, when you do the Warrior Two pose, your instructor can actually read your mind. Well, not really, but they can tell if you're leaning forward that you're thinking about your future and if you're leaning backward that you're thinking about the past. Just another example of your thoughts having physical effects.

If, however, your posture is straight, then you are fully in the moment. So there's the first way you can learn what being in the moment feels like. If you don't know what the Warrior Two pose looks like, I can almost guarantee you've seen it before and it'll come up right away in a quick online search. Go ahead and do the pose now, being aware of centering your posture. I'll wait.

What was your first instinct when you did it? Were you leaning forward: worrying about your to-do list, or leaning backward: regretting and stressing over the past? How did your mind change when you consciously straightened yourself? If you want to, try again with these questions in mind.

Now that you know what it feels like to be in the moment, what do you do here? Anxiety is worry. Worry is the future, so in order to get into the present moment and stay there, you might want a distraction. You have plenty of options here, and you can use them whether you're at home or in the car.

The Art of Distraction

It's as simple as having a hobby and doing something you love. What do you enjoy? Are you crafty? A reader? Do you enjoy knitting? Bring those things along with you (as long as you're not the one driving) and do them in the car. You'll have the added benefit of not realizing the time as it passes, so the trip will even seem shorter.

And this isn't limited to long road trips. If you want to knit in the car on the way to the grocery store or the movie theater, you do it. Play three levels of your favorite game on your phone. This is your life, and no one can judge you for what works for you.

But what if you're the driver? I hear you. I can't stand long car rides because I end up feeling trapped and bored (same thing, if you ask me). My favorite solution here is music. There is nothing like an excellent playlist to get you jamming out. I had a special playlist for driving before my husband and I lived together. At the time, he lived in Virginia while I lived in Pennsylvania and it was a six-hour journey to visit him. But the destination was worth it and the music was good, so I made it safely every time.

My husband still employs this tactic for me when we drive to Virginia together to visit his family. He made the ultimate sacrifice and now every time we get in the car for a long trip, 90's boy bands serenade us for most, if not all of the way, and I am the fan in the front row belting the songs with all my heart.

And you know what? I don't freak out anymore. I even occasionally let him change the station to something else more often than I used to.

Music is magic and it will bring you into the moment.

Another great distraction is other people. Why go alone when you can bring someone along to keep you in the moment with great conversation, even if it's through the hands-free setting on your cell phone? You don't have to go through anything on your own, and it can begin in the car, especially as you're getting used to driving again.

Managing a Panic Attack

Perhaps the best physical tool for managing an anxiety attack is breathing. Have you ever had one of those moments where you become weirdly aware of your own breathing? You start to breathe weirdly because you're thinking about it, but you could use this to your benefit instead. Deep breaths really do calm you down. They're not always easy, and I know you've probably heard this before, but they work.

When you feel anxiety coming on, here is your game plan:

- Talk out loud. Count, recite your ABC's, say some positive affirmations like "I am safe," "I can breathe," or sing. The slower you do this, the better, because you're already amped to go too fast. Show your brain that slow is the way to go. It distracts the brain from thinking about the bad stuff.
- Do something with your hands, even if it's just drumming a slow and steady beat on the steering wheel.

- Let yourself laugh if you feel silly doing any of this.
- Breathe in through your nose and out through your mouth until your body calms itself down (remember, it's just trying to save your life).
- Then, finally, my cherry on top: List three things you're grateful for even if they're weird things, like I'm grateful that I get to have pizza later today. I'm grateful that I woke up this morning. I'm grateful that I can do anything I set my mind to. Gratitude is the feeling you have when you're living in the moment. It's love, which is the realest thing in the world.

These simple things will draw you back into the present. Because what is a panic attack? It's a flight reaction. You've heard about fight or flight. Well, you can't run away when you're in the car, so your brain resorts to a mental getaway. It freaks out as a way of escaping the moment. It releases chemicals that pump up your adrenaline because it thinks you should either be running or swinging your fists. So you can expect those chemicals to run their course, but the more you allow the fear to continue, the more fear hormones your body sends out. You just have to switch gears.

I want you to understand something. Love is real. Fear is fake. Fear is all about the "what if." *What if something goes wrong? What if I get hurt? What if [insert your worry here]?* Gratitude, like we used above, is real. It's love. It's joy. It shows you what's true and calms you down so you can have a clear perspective. Fear just makes things seem worse than they are, and I can prove it.

Have you ever gone into a situation that you were afraid of, and when it was over you released the breath you were holding the whole time and found yourself saying, "Well that wasn't so bad?" That's because the fear only made you *think* it would be bad, and it manifested a harder time for you than you needed. Once you got into the moment – where you have control – it was fine because you could handle it.

Solutions Outside of the Car

What about before or in between drives? How can you condition yourself to be cool and collected even before you sit in the car? The world is your oyster here, and you can choose what works for you. What I love most is understanding the energy in and around me. It's another way to bring myself into the moment whether it's on a drive, in a public place, or all by my lonesome.

You've probably heard of Reiki and energy healing. Reiki is a therapy that can be performed by a practitioner, but you can also do it for yourself. Use meditation to simply become aware of the tingly or warm feeling all around you (that's what energy feels like), and picture it in balance. Boom. Intro to Reiki that you can use right now.

If you'd rather have a professional help you out, it's getting easier and easier to find a practitioner in your area, but always choose someone you feel safe with. Much like hypnotism, you are meant to allow your mind to relax when receiving Reiki or any energy therapy, so if you're not vibing with the practitioner, it may not be as helpful of a session.

Another factor you may not have expected to contribute to anxiety is your nutrition. It turns out that healthy foods can regulate the stress chemicals in your body and help to bring your energy in balance, so if Reiki and other energy therapies like IET and the ThetaHealing® Technique are a little too woo-woo for you, simply balancing your nutrition with vegetables and noninflammatory foods (another easy list to find on Pinterest) is a practical way to do the trick.

Food is the instinctual way that our bodies like to bring us back to the moment and "ground" ourselves. I've had several intuitive mentors warn me about watching what I eat because overeating helped me feel grounded.

When you're feeling bored or anxious, do you find yourself craving something to help curb the stress? Eating is another way to live in the moment, to be honest. Sure, I'm a nutrition coach and I take fueling my body seriously, but don't think for one second that I don't enjoy food.

They say you should eat slowly because it helps you know when you're full so you don't overeat. That's accurate, but I eat slowly because I don't want the eating to end! I enjoy the moment of whatever the food is – especially when it happens to be chocolate cake or Chinese takeout.

Choose your food wisely around eighty percent of the time (#treatyourself) and not only will you bring your mind back to the moment, but you'll be giving your body something that helps it feel safe enough not to need anxiety in the first place. This may also lead to weight loss, which could be an added perk if that happens to be another goal of yours.

The bottom line for preventing a panic attack is living the lifestyle of someone who doesn't have panic attacks. You already know what she looks like. She's the fearless woman.

It's manifesting, like we talked about in chapter four. It's being that person who doesn't have time to panic because they're too busy nurturing themselves, enjoying their hobbies, and living life to the fullest, with the occasional #nofilter photo to post on social media as proof that you have those amazing moments in your life too.

Fill your life with things that bring you joy and don't leave space for anxiety. When you're in the car, occupy yourself with music, with focus on the road as the person who is in control and can adapt to whatever potholes life throws at her. If you live a life like that, anxiety won't fit in, and you won't have to deal with it anymore. You understand your divine timing, you created your trip before you even got in the car, so now all that's left is to enjoy going through the motions of getting there. You are an organized, bliss-seeking boss woman who is in control of her circumstances.

Control is everything. Control makes us feel safe. When we don't have control is when we start to have problems. But you already know how to handle the things you can't control, and I challenge you to remember that when you start to feel worried. Remember your divine timing, use your tools, and if it still starts to make you panic, use the techniques and tools we just covered to get through the fear and back into the moment. Thank your brain for wanting to protect you, but let it know you've got this and everything will be fine. Because it will be.

And if you need support doing that, you can always find help through coaching or Reiki or just a good, supportive friend.

Rest Stop: Your Practical Prevention Checklist

Let's consider what this looks like for you, personally. Use the page below to make a list of the ideas you have for managing and preventing your anxiety in the best, most enjoyable ways. Anything to add to my suggestions?

Record them in your journal! Doodle all over it. Make it fun!

- What hobbies do you enjoy outside of the car or while in the passenger seat?
- What food are you going to buy this week to set your body up for less stress?
- What's your favorite way to live in the moment?
- What is your plan to handle a panic attack if it happens again?
- Bonus: Do the Warrior Two pose again and write down whether you lean forward, backward, or upright!

Chapter Seven:

Anxiety Triggers and How to Stop Them

When you think about what triggers your panic attacks, what do you come up with? Is it a random tire squeal from another car? Driving too fast? Hitting the breaks too hard? Another car not stopping quickly enough at a stop sign?

If you could name the first thing that comes to your mind, what would it be?

It can honestly be anything, but it all traces back to the same root: fear. "I'm afraid of…" And what are you supposed to do with that? Too often, that feels like the end of the line, the dead end that offers no solution. Fear is natural, so how are you supposed to challenge it?

It may not seem like it, but fear is manageable. Fear is one of the things that you *can* control. You just never had permission to think that way before, but now you do.

Facing Your Fears

"Courage was not the absence of fear, but the triumph over it. The brave man is not he who does not feel afraid, but he who conquers that fear."
–NELSON MANDELA

If fear was the girl you see in the mirror, would you regard her with hate? Fear is the child in you that doesn't want to get hurt again. There's nothing wrong with feeling that way, but you're reading this book because you want to move past that fear. You want to feel like you're in control again, without panic attacks.

Let's look at this from a black and white perspective: if you are the hero, anxiety is your villain. How does this villain get the best of you? What is it about panic that challenges you enough to make you struggle?

Does a word come up for you when you think about it? What is it the fear of?

You may be tempted to say, "I don't know." And you'd be right. It's okay not to know. If you knew, you wouldn't be so afraid. With anxiety, it's always a future scenario. *What if...? If I drive again, I might have another accident.*

The fear of the unknown is the root trigger for your anxiety. It's the worry of what *might* be. You already know what is and what was, and you survived all of that, so it's what *could* be that scares your brain into thinking it's not worth trying to drive in the first place. When you look to the future, you can imagine infinite possibilities, and it's impossible to choose which one will happen.

It's all out of your control.

That sounds like a dead end. So what can you do about it? How can you find your villain's weakness and defeat it?

Let's start from the outside and work our way in. How can you feel safe in the world around you?

Making Magic

I used to work at Disney World, the most magical place on earth, and the thing you don't expect when going "Behind the Magic" is how much Disney focuses on creating a safe space for their guests. The first things we learned were the traditions that made Disney the company it is today and how that company has one priority: the guest experience, beginning with safety. We had a phrase drilled into our heads from day one: "Safe-D begins with me!"

One of my trainers told us that Disney World intentionally creates a space that seems untouched and disconnected from the outside world. They want guests to feel like they don't have to worry about anything, and it's the cast members' job to keep that "show" going. So when someone would carelessly run over our feet with a stroller, we were encouraged to remember that they felt safe enough not to have to check their surroundings, which meant we were succeeding at doing our job.

Have you ever visited a place like that? A place where you could let your guard down, breathe deep, and not worry about having control over everything?

Disney does a fantastic job of controlling their environment and creating a reality that is safe and even magical for everyone involved. Yes. I worked there and I still believe Disney is a great company, at least as far as my experience with it goes.

So how can we add a touch of that same magic to your life? How can you control your environment? What does that look like without a multi-million-dollar budget to build your own amusement park getaway?

Let's start with the obvious: you. The environment and everything you experience comes from you, as we discussed in chapter four, so it all begins with you. You already understand the concept of manifesting, but let's go more tangible. There are two ways to understand a situation, and if you're going to be your own hero, you need to know your strengths, know your weaknesses, and understand how to flip the script to use your resources to your advantage.

I'll share a secret with you. Your weaknesses are just as fake as fear is.

Imagine your flaws are the heads side of a coin. Flip the coin and rewrite that flaw. What I expect you to realize is, that flaw becomes a strength.

Flaws are nothing more than our strengths getting carried away.

So when someone calls me impatient, or when I put myself down for being impatient, I can remind myself that I'm just being extremely driven, and maybe more driven than the situation calls for.

When someone says you're arrogant or self-centered, or you feel like you might be considered arrogant even though you're not insulting or hurting anyone, that's because you appreciate yourself. That's golden. Don't lose that!

If you're lazy, you actually just understand the value of rest.

See what I mean?

You are intentional. And I can just about guarantee that those strengths are represented somewhere in your astrological birth chart like we talked about in chapter five.

So what causes you to focus so much on your weaknesses and therefore allow fear to run the show and bring on anxiety?

Doubt and fear. Every time. Those two emotions are the true villains to your hero, and you don't need to acknowledge them, because they are the causes of panic and stress and anxiety. They are what make you believe that the next time you get in a car, you're going to freak out because freaking out is who you are: your weakness.

Flip the coin on anxiety and what do you get? Any answer that comes to you is valid and it's entirely yours. When I flip the coin, I get control. I choose to exercise this control in a healthy way through co-creation. By focusing my intentions on manifesting positive things that are within my realm of control, and respecting my personal divine timing as a foundation to build those intentions upon, I create a life that feels confident, safe, and magical.

The Key to Confidence

Let me ask you another question and follow it up with some good news that might blow your mind. Does being confident feel safe? Or are you worried that acting confident will cause people to make fun of you? Have you experienced that weird situation where you say something positive about yourself and someone always has to scoff at you and tear you down for being "arrogant?"

I'll be the first to tell you this, in case no one has yet – You. Are. Not. Arrogant.

You are beautiful. You are magic. And they are afraid.

I don't believe it's possible to be arrogant while you're also choosing to love yourself and others. Arrogance is a defense mechanism that comes from fear. Confidence is a strength that gets you out of your own way so you can show up for yourself and for others. It's a way of knowing what you're capable of so you can put your strengths to good use. Insecurity forces you to hide in the corner, and who are you going to help from way over there?

I choose to understand myself and know myself so I can control my reactions to unexpected, uncontrollable situations. If I want to fix myself or help fix something with someone else, I need to know what tools I have at my disposal, to know that I'm the right and most capable person for the job. This is how you can be sure of what you love doing, this is how you can find your fit, the place where you feel valued and safe, the strength to get behind a wheel and feel in control regardless of what may come at you. Confidence is your magical amusement park where you can feel at ease instead of uncomfortable.

I don't know about you, but I'm not going to spend my free time in a place that doesn't feel safe. And that's okay. There is a time and a place for saying no.

If I know that I don't like being in a certain type of situation, I don't need to put myself in that situation to begin with. It's okay to say no.

However, if I don't like being in a certain situation because fear or anxiety ruin it for me, that's a different story. My mom *could have* fed a lion. She wishes she had. She taught me that I deserve joy, and I'm restricting my potential by allowing fear to guide me.

You can know the difference. You already do. If you feel like you're missing out on something you'd love, then accept the challenge and grow. Situations are only uncomfortable until they aren't. That is to say, you only feel uncomfortable doing a thing or being in a place for as long as it takes for that experience to become familiar and part of your comfort zone. That's growth. That's a good thing. Growth comes from a place of love, and love gives you the motivation and the courage to grow.

If love is the energy of God/the Universe/Source, then that's the energy I want to follow. That's the energy I want to put behind my responses to everything. That's the foundation I want to build my world upon.

When I think of controlling any situation, I think of choosing to act and react out of love rather than fear. If I do that, then I know my strengths and my confidence will always outweigh my flaws.

So when you get behind the wheel next, get in that car focused on having a lovely drive, not a terrifying one.

Get in the car with confidence, expecting that it will go smoothly because you are capable.

Don't worry about what might happen. Decide what *will* happen. Worrying is the future, and worrying about something isn't going to stop it from happening, especially if it's divine timing. Worrying will only blind you to your options, and worse, it puts you through the bad situation twice. By imagining going through another accident, you're feeling the same fears and traumas of actually having that accident. Why would you want to put yourself through that more times than you have to?

Why would you want to look back even after a bad thing and realize that, while you could have been happy, you chose to be afraid?

Anxiety is a physical reaction, so I won't try to undervalue you by saying "it's a choice." Even if that's somewhat true, it doesn't help you. What does help is understanding your options.

You already know that anxiety is a process your body goes through to keep you safe. Love your body for that. It means well, but you can also train your body to feel safe anyway. Give your brain its own amusement park environment by setting the scene in a way that feels so magical it isn't even the "real" world.

You're not fooling yourself here, you're manifesting a new, better reality. And you have nothing to lose. At the very least, if something does go wrong, you only have to experience it once rather than worrying about it countless times when it may never actually happen at all.

One of my favorite quotes is:

"What if I fall? Oh, but my darling, what if you fly?"
—ERIN HANSEN

Why do we allow ourselves to be so caught up on what could go wrong – making space for that reality to come to pass – instead of what could go wonderfully?

I say this a lot, but that's because it's important: Your thoughts create your reality. You can't control all of your thoughts, but you can retrain your brain to react differently. You can catch yourself and redirect your mental energy to something positive. You can take the scary thought like "what if I have another car accident?" and flip the coin to "what if I'm an amazing driver and this is the best trip of my life?"

Which would you rather experience twice? The excitement or the fear? Even if you set yourself up for the excitement and end up receiving the fear (which shouldn't happen often if you use divine timing), you'll only have to experience the fear once and you'll have enough energy to pick yourself up and keep moving because you didn't drain yourself with constant anxiety.

You can heal the thing that causes your brain to go haywire in the first place: your emotions. Choosing your thoughts, re-framing them when necessary, is a huge step. Believe it or not, you don't control your own thoughts as much as you think you do. Your thoughts are triggered by the feelings you get in certain situations. And those feelings are determined the very first time you experience that situation, which could have been ages ago when you were a child and your brain was still in a constant Theta state, but you're still running that outdated version of the software. To a seven-year-old, losing a balloon is traumatic. Do you still want or need that fear? What you need is a software update. That's where choosing your thoughts comes in.

You can stop your panic attacks with the same thing that gives them power: your mind. It's all about a sense of control. Your brain doesn't feel in control, so it starts doing what any good brain would do. It generates scenarios, but since it had a bad experience before, and since it was a first experience, the brain only wants to help you survive, so it wants you to avoid what it believes threatened you before. That's just instinct. But you're more than your instincts. You're a confident, reasoning, miraculous, intentional blend of love and stardust. You are magic.

Rest Stop: The Coin Toss

Here's an exercise I call the Coin Toss:

Make a list in your journal of your weaknesses. Go ahead, pick on yourself for a minute, but don't go crazy. Stop at ten, and try not to go that far to begin with.

Now, look at your list. How does it make you feel? I'm guessing not great. But these things you notice about yourself, these flaws that you can't help but see first when you look yourself in the face every morning, are an illusion created by fear and doubt to keep you from taking risks and owning your magic, standing in your power.

Go back to your list and rewrite your flaws into strengths. Cross out the weaknesses. They aren't real. Then add this to everything you understand about yourself so far from this book, and look at the masterpiece you're unveiling!

Chapter Eight:

Teach Your Brain Not to Panic

The most ridiculous thing I've ever heard came from the first counselor I opened up to about my experiences with an abusive relationship. It took me three years to realize that I wasn't to blame for what happened to me, and I did what I thought was the mature thing to do and sought out help.

It only took two sessions of me telling him what he wanted to hear before he told me I had done most of the work on my own and I no longer needed him. I was fine with that because I felt that I was the one counseling him more than anything, but above all else was the theme of my sessions with him. It always came back to these phrases. Maybe you've heard them too.

"Understand, you are the victim," and "you will live with this [PTSD, depression, anxiety] for the rest of your life. There is no fixing it."

I call shenanigans. I refuse to sit around anticipating my next flashback or anxiety attack and just accepting it with an, "Oh well, guess I'm just broken and that's the way things are."

The crux of the issue is that, while there are tangible, physical ways to find healing as we discussed in chapter six, much of the healing is emotional. Your mind, your feelings, your heart – those are the things that were wounded most. They need to heal, but as with a sprained ankle, if you keep walking on it, then it doesn't have the opportunity to rest and heal correctly.

Your anxiety attacks in the car may be uncomfortable, but they *are* curable, you just don't have the best methods to cope with them – yet! You can drive without a panic attack. You did it before the accident. You know what it feels like to drive safely and breathe normally the whole way through.

Your Feelings Started It

The trick to emotionally healing your anxiety comes back to something that I've hinted at before and that sounds simple: emotions.

When you have an experience for the first time, your brain records it and bases every similar situation from that moment forward off of that first experience. What happens if the brain sets a standard with a bad experience? It decides that situations that feel similar are unsafe for you, and it panics to get you out of there to keep you alive.

Thank you, Brain, but no. That kind of thing was necessary when we were more nomadic and faced threats in the wild or whatever, but these days I don't need to trigger a fight or flight reaction just driving to get my morning coffee. There is no vicious animal waiting to pounce, but your brain doesn't realize that on an instinctual level.

When I talk about healing holistically, I mean healing on every level: mind, body, and soul. We figured out the body in the last chapter, now we're going to talk about mind, and don't worry, we'll get to the soul part too in chapter ten.

How can you retrain your brain to stop feeling like your morning commute is going to be the end of you? The same way you would help a friend or family member relax: try and understand *why* it feels that way.

Where do feelings come from? Feelings are reactions. They are your front line when dealing with the world. You already understand this because you can walk into a room and know if something is up. You can look at someone and tell, "Oh, Carol's not in a good mood today." You can stand at the edge of a cliff (with a bungee, please) and realize, "I don't have a good feeling about this."

You know feelings. You just didn't know that they are the foundation of everything you experience, think, and create around you.

Feelings trigger thoughts. This is why you shouldn't feel bad when you think something negative about yourself or other people. It doesn't mean you aren't nice, it just means that the feeling you have in that moment triggered a weird thought. So think again. Change the thought from whatever the negative phrase was into a positive one, and your actions will change too.

When you get in the car, the feeling you have based on the fear from your accident triggers thoughts like, *I'm not going to make it through this drive. I can't do this,* and then your body acts on that thought by panicking.

It's okay that you think that way. You can give yourself a little grace and forgive yourself for that. Just don't let it stop there. Change the thought. Talk to yourself and adjust the phrase. *I'm excited for my morning coffee. Traffic is light. I can do anything.* Throw a bit of sass in there if helps: *Excuse me, Brain, but I've got this. You can relax now. We're okay.* Again, your body will react accordingly.

Do you ever take it to that step, or do you tend to agree with your brain, allow anxiety to overcome you, and retreat back to your house?

Remember this: if you aren't happy, it isn't over. That applies to every situation. If you get in the car and you aren't happy, then adjust something until you are, and you'll feel safe enough to pull out of the driveway. Let your destination motivate you, or even the successful conquering of your fears.

Muscle Testing

To heal your anxiety attacks on an emotional level, we're going to rebuild the emotions you have toward driving from ones of panic and fear to ones of experience and confidence. I'll talk about specific tools, both physical ones you can use daily and more mental/spiritual ones you can use to retrain your brain in the coming chapters, but for now, I want to shine a spotlight on what a practical approach to emotional healing looks like.

Have you ever heard of kinesiology or muscle testing? You can find videos about how to do it on the internet but in short, it's using your muscles to see what your subconscious really feels or believes.

There are a few ways to do it. One of the most common and easiest to describe practices is sticking your arm straight out in front of you and calibrating your answers by saying "Yes" then having someone try to push your arm down. If you are hydrated and your energy is balanced, your arm will firmly resist. If not, drink some water. It helps trick your body into thinking it's hydrated.

Then try again, but say "No" and this time when your partner pushes on your arm, it will suddenly go weak and fall. It's a crazy feeling, but now you have something to show you proof of what your subconscious believes, and you'll be able to understand how that affects you.

Try saying phrases like, "I am safe in the car," and see what your arm says. Is it a yes or a no?

In the ThetaHealing® Technique and Integrated Energy Therapy, we take it further by finding out how deep the belief runs so we can heal it instantly, but in this case, since you had the accident, we can be almost certain it's on what's called a core or physical level of belief. Something you learned to believe in this lifetime based on your experiences, and there are options to simply change the belief on your own by rephrasing it like we discussed before.

If your arm tells you "no, you aren't safe," then all you have to do is close your eyes and say it again, allowing yourself to believe it. Say it multiple times if it helps. Tell your brain what's what. It'll listen. If it doesn't, don't worry. Just keep reading. You'll find more ways to do this in chapter ten.

Follow God Through Your Fear

The source of my anxiety has always been the plain and simple fear of death. Talk about deep levels of belief. No one ever had to explain to me what death was because I was panicking about it as soon as I could talk. To remedy this, I actually went through a past life regression. Now, I'm not here to sell you on reincarnation. It wasn't the past lives that helped me most, it was what the practitioner guided me to do.

As she walked me through each past life scenario, she would take me straight to the moment of my death in that lifetime. She asked me to keep following the story through and *beyond* death.

I died in the surgery I mentioned in chapter two. You'd think my fear would be moot after that, but I didn't get to see the glorious white light people talk about, so I was terrified during the regression that I'd just see black nothingness and that all my fears would be confirmed, but that wasn't the case at all. It wasn't even what I saw that helped me.

As you can probably guess, it's what I felt.

Calm, relaxed, rested, at peace, without stress. I don't feel that way often. That's one of the only times in my life I can remember truly having nothing to stress or worry about. Can you think of a time like that? Do you know what that feels like? It's okay if you don't. That's part of why you're here, and I have hope for you.

A theme that comes up with a lot of my clients is what I've come to call "following God through your fear."

I deal a lot with divine timing. My intuition revolves around it, and when things are going against divine timing, I get alarms to the point that I am compelled to intervene, so when clients come to me and their divine timing is at risk, the same message comes up: you have to trust that if what you're afraid of most is what God knows is best, then it will turn out all right. You have to be willing to follow God *through* your fear, the same way I had to go through death in my past life regressions. I just needed to face it and see what transformation waited for me on the other side of the fear.

You're afraid of the feeling you get when you're driving. No one can blame you for that, and I'm not here to try and make you feel bad about it. That would only create more issues for you. I'm not here to validate you as a victim either. What I want is to walk with you through your fear so you don't have to do it alone. I want you to see what's on the other side because it's going to allow you to breathe and rest and feel joy again without restraint.

The best way to heal your panic attacks is to heal your heart. Heal your feelings so that your mind can rest knowing you are safe. You can feel at ease and drive anywhere and make memories and enjoy your life to the fullest because you didn't come into this world to be average or to let fear be your guide.

You came here to be awesome!

Look again at the list of strengths you made in the last chapter. You. *Are*. Awesome. Everything about you is a strength or a talent. Are you able to express them to their fullest right now with anxiety holding you back?

I want you to *feel* better. Because I know that then you will *think* better. You'll be able to act however *you* choose to. And you will realize how awesome your life is and how awesome you are.

And driving in a car will be a walk in the park.

Forgive Your Feelings

Your feelings are valid. They aren't stupid. They happen for a very scientific reason, and now you realize it's not your fault. So the next thing I want you to understand is forgiveness.

Yes, really. Can you honestly tell me that you aren't hard on yourself every day? Would you be able to look me in the eye and say that without flinching? If we muscle tested it – by the way, go ahead and do that – would it come out that yes, you forgive yourself for the accident and your anxiety?

Fear causes negative emotions. It causes anger and resentment, and I'll bet my left arm this has happened to you. But you can change it. If you forgive your mind and your body for putting you through all this exhausting crap, you will be able to heal. That twinge in your chest when you picture yourself in a car will go away.

All you have to do is say it out loud, and do it until it feels like you mean it. Say it while looking in the mirror so you can make eye contact. Make it a daily routine.

Your mind is simply trying to protect you. Your body is reacting to the signals your brain sends out. They are helping you in the only ways they know how. Thank them for it and bless them. Let them know you're safe and they've done their job.

And, yes, I'm asking you to talk to your body. This can help with all sorts of things, including your confidence, which will leave even less space in your life for your anxiety.

Do Your Research

Now you know how to fix your emotional trauma, but how can you prevent something like this from happening again? Do your research. You don't need to read any more books, you've already got this one and I'm not going to set you up to have to build a library of self-help books on the exact same subject.

I want you to start with something as simple as your favorite color.

Knowing what you believe and what you value is your power. That's where confidence comes from. It makes you unshakable.

Have you ever had a debate with someone? You go back and forth, arguing your own points until they pull out a question that you don't have the answer to because you don't have any knowledge or experience to support an opinion. It happened to me too often, so I decided I wanted to know myself and what I believed so that if someone questioned me, I wouldn't try to change their mind – that's not the goal – but I *would* be able to stand up for myself enough to not question everything *I* believe in.

Everyone is entitled to their own opinions, wouldn't you agree? So what are yours?

Who are you when it comes to driving a car? Are you the woman who panics on the drive, and that's just the way it is? I won't judge you for that, but you may want to return this book if that's the case. Or are you the woman who drives like Marilyn Monroe and lives her life the same way, indulging in every moment, comfortable in her own skin, and not needing approval from anyone but herself?

When you are that woman, the fearless woman, panic doesn't have a place anymore. Panic is the person on the other side of the argument here. Are you going to let it win, or are you going to take the question that stumped you, research it, and find your answer?

"Driving isn't safe," your panic tells you.

"Yes, it is," you counter.

"Why?"

Why? When you get to the journal page at the end of this chapter, write down why driving is safe. Heck, write it in the margins of this page or on a note in your phone. Make your reasons why driving is safe the background on your phone so you see it every time you look down.

Driving is safe. You know from back in chapter five that if it were your time to go, you'd be gone. But your accident wasn't your time and today isn't either.

So, really then, if you understand your divine timing and you understand that you have so much purpose in life – what do you have to be afraid of? On any given day, you are going to be faced with two things: your own choices and divine timing. You understand that you have the power to use both to your advantage, so nothing can hurt you. And if things do get hard, you know to look for meaning in them rather than allowing them to create fear in you.

You have too much to do in this life to leave space for anxiety. You have places to be and your car will get you there in one beautiful, strong, and confident piece. Are you going to let fear of all things stand in your way?

Fear is nothing but an enemy for you to conquer so you can understand your true greatness. Fear isn't what you think it is.

Flip the Script on Fear

What if I told you the accident did you a favor like I suggested a few chapters ago? I saved this question because, by now, you've read enough of this book to know I'm on your side, but I do believe the accident helped you.

One of the worst things that have ever happened to me was an abusive relationship. It wrecked me and led to three years of rebuilding myself and dealing with anxiety and flashbacks I was told I'd just have to live with. I'd never, ever repeat those years. But I also wouldn't change or erase them. They forced me to tear down a version of me who allowed people to treat her like dirt. They gave me space to do my research and decide who I am, what I stand for, what I believe. I recreated myself from those ashes and I never would have done it otherwise.

That relationship and the few years that followed were arduous, but I understand how they served me. I am incredible thanks to the lessons they taught me, and you can claim a victory from your accident as well.

Since we're all about flipping the script on your beliefs in this chapter, how did the accident help you? What has it shown you that you didn't realize before?

How is the panic serving you? We know your body thinks the panic is keeping you safe, but is that all there is to it? Or is there something that was missing in your life before that you have now?

I've worked with many clients who created an illness for themselves because they needed rest, or wanted to feel loved and felt like they needed an excuse to ask for it.

Is there a void in your life that the anxiety helps you fill? If there is, don't get upset with yourself. Remember we're all about forgiveness here. But now you know. You've done your research and you can fill that space in a better, more positive way. Like telling your husband you'd like to have more date nights, or learning to say "thank you, but I'm staying in tonight" when your friends ask you out but you don't feel like going because fuzzy socks are more your speed that night.

It's entirely possible that the anxiety is giving you a reason to say no to things you don't want to do.

Rest Stop: Do Your Research

Muscle test yourself for these things and record your answers in your journal:

- "My favorite color is _____."
- "I am allowed to say no."
- "I am loved."
- "I love myself."
- "My anxiety serves me." (Why? Test for that as well so you have tangible proof!)
- "Driving is safe" (Why? Don't lose the argument with your brain!)

- "I forgive myself for the accident."

Was the answer "no" to any of those? I have a surprise for you…

That's *phenomenal*! Good!

I am thrilled for you, and I'll tell you why. You understand now. You get it. You have found the thing that you need to fix. It's out in the open, so guess what happens next?

We're going to help you fix it, once and for all. You've just cracked the code of how to heal yourself and that means you are ready for the rest of this book to show you how to change your fears into strengths with real tools you can actually use.

I'm *proud* of you.

Chapter Nine:

What to Do When You Don't Feel Like Fighting

The first thing I want you to understand before we go any further is that you should be proud of yourself. You should be excited. You know what needs fixing and that is ninety percent of the problem.

Now we get to the solution. Not just the ones that help you heal, but the ones you can track every day to prove to yourself that you're making progress. There shouldn't be any guesswork here. No matter what your energy level is like on a given day, you are covered and predestined for success.

I mentioned before that healing your anxiety happens on physical and emotional levels, so we're going to start from the surface and dig our way down.

Realistically, you may not wake up every day eager to exert the mental and emotional effort of fighting anxiety. So I want to equip you with physical tools to use as part of your daily routine first. You have plenty of resources. Even if you choose to use only physical tools, you are still setting yourself up for success, and if you take it a step further to the spiritual and emotional tools we'll talk about in the next chapter, you'll be even more unstoppable and see even faster results.

First, I want you to think about what a typical day in your life looks like. That's where everything has to start. You need to make space in your life for getting better, and the bonus is these techniques will never get old. You can use them to keep joy in your life and solve any problem from this moment on. They can become a permanent part of your routine and you'll never step aside for fear to come back into your life again. It's a lifestyle change, but an easy one, and it's a permanent solution.

You can do any of these things on their own, or you can do several of them at once, because I understand a boss woman needs to be able to multitask.

Manage Your Time

With that in mind, a good way to understand your day is to plan it out. Do you have a planner? If not, use the bullet journal pages in this book as your new bonus planner.

Managing your time is often overlooked, but when you know what to expect, the fear of the unknown doesn't have a slot in your day. This is also a great way to tangibly practice manifesting. Simply setting the intention that at 8 a.m., you're going to do yoga for half an hour and focus on your breathing and relaxation physically creates space for that in your life, and gives you the time and permission to do exactly that. Anything that would normally get in the way can be scheduled for another time, because you know what your day looks like.

You can even track your astrological transits and make note of the numerological number each day so you have an idea of what your divine timing looks like for that day. Can you imagine seeing your schedule, your divine timing, and the intentions you have for everything in your day all in one place? How does that level of control and peace of mind feel for you? That's exactly what I'm giving you in these final Rest Stop exercises.

A planner is the most basic way to take control of your life, and there are so many ways to integrate your personal divine timing and positivity into your day so you are ready for anything and making space for success in co-creation with God.

Another thing to make space for in your schedule is some sort of physical routine like the yoga at 8 a.m. Start your day with movement to release any pent-up energy, and relax your body for the day ahead. Yoga is known as a form of moving meditation, so if you wish you could meditate but you just can't sit still, yoga will naturally help you balance your energy, relax, and strengthen your body all at once. Now that's multitasking!

Take it a step further with all facets of your day by writing an intention down for everything you're doing today. Meeting at 10 a.m.? Next to that, write how you intend for the meeting to go. How will you feel during that meeting? Prepared and responsive?

How about the drive to work? Put it in your planner and write your intention for the drive. If you're not sure how to possibly make an intention that big happen, that's fine. Set a smaller intention. You don't need to write that you're going to get through the drive without any anxiety at all. Be kind to yourself and accept how you feel. Instead, try to work the big goals backward.

If you want to stop having anxiety, what has to come first? You need to breathe normally, you need to feel calm. How does that happen? Is it having a bottle of water in the car or the perfect music station on the radio? Work it back and back again until you have a small, manageable step to do regularly and before you know it, you've mastered driving again.

Try writing: *9:30 a.m. - Drive to work. I feel calm and breathe normally the entire drive.*

You're not demanding that your subconscious stop panicking right now, you're just asking your body to breathe. That's something it already knows how to do. Deep, normal breaths to keep your body functioning can actually cut the panic reaction short, so use your breathing to your advantage. Claim it and make space for it.

Again, manifesting is not an abstract concept. It's how you live your life. Every goal you set for yourself is an intention. It's the follow-through that brings it into reality.

Creating these routines and doing them regularly gives you a sense of what to expect each day and therefore less to worry about.

Organize Your Space

Another way you can focus on creating a safe space for yourself like we discussed in chapter six is to de-clutter or organize the space that gives you the most anxiety. Is your car clean and organized? If you get pulled over or need something in your car, do you know where it is so you won't panic trying to find it?

Remember, you don't have to do this alone. Sometimes just facing the task of organizing is difficult, but if you do it with a friend or partner, you have the support to help you get through it, and all you have to do after that is keep it organized so you'll never have to do a deep clean again.

What about your anxiety levels before getting in the car? Does a messy kitchen drive you nuts like it does for me? Let your house and your car be your personal Disney World, where nothing from the outside can stress you out and everything inside feels safe and magical. You'll be clearing the energy in your house at the same time, so you'll notice it actually does *feel* better.

Journaling

The most effective tool I've found is journaling, and you may have noticed I've been setting you up for this one throughout most of the book. Journaling isn't just about writing out your feelings. It's about getting the stuff in your head out and onto paper where you can either let it go – that tricky final step of manifesting – or read it objectively to find solutions.

What I like to do with journaling is vent. I'm an expert venter. When I get frustrated, nothing moves forward until I get to describe exactly how unfair a situation is and why it makes no sense for it to be happening to me in the first place. Most of the time, I already know what I *should* do, but I'm not going to do it until I can complain about it first. It's okay to have a process that works for you, no matter what other people might think of it.

Journaling is a safe space to throw an adult tantrum without worrying about people judging you for it. If I need to vent in order to disperse anxious energy and take control of a situation, then that's what I'm going to do. That's my process and everyone deserves their process.

What does your process look like? Don't limit yourself because of what others might think. Some people don't understand dipping sandwich cookies in peanut butter, but that doesn't make it taste any less delicious to the people who enjoy it. It makes those people unique. Your process is uniquely yours, and that's fine. Can you imagine a world where we are all the same, the way social media makes us think it should be? Take a step back and really picture that for a moment. Why would the world need seven billion carbon copies of the same personality? Nothing would ever get accomplished! So in the same way you accept others for what they choose to do with their lives, accept yourself and figure out what works for you. Do the research we mentioned in chapter eight and decide what you prefer. Write it in your journal pages to figure it out.

Journaling is also a great way to ask questions and actually get answers. When I'm writing a fiction story and I run into writers' block, I pull out a notebook and simply ask the question "What happens next?" Then I write down everything that comes to my mind. Every possibility. Inevitably, one idea will spring off into a bunch of other ideas and voila, I have a story.

Life is just like a story. So when the plot confuses you, sit down with your journal and simply ask yourself what happens next, or "Why am I feeling this way?" See what comes to mind and, at the very least, you'll realize one thing you might have forgotten: you always have options. Everything in your life is a choice. You can choose to stay where you are or you can choose to change. And you can know specifically how to do it.

When clients come to me for depression or anxiety, this is one of my favorite homework assignments to give them because they always come back knowing the problem *and* how to fix it in their own unique way.

You may recall I mentioned you learned most of your beliefs before you were seven years old, when your brain was in its constant theta brain wave that we use in the ThetaHealing® Technique. Like I said before, to a seven-year-old, losing a balloon can feel like loss and abandonment, and that's what you're basing the rest of your life upon! If you constantly feel alone and don't know why, ask your inner seven-year-old, "Why do I constantly feel alone?" and see what answers you write down. Open your mind without judgment and let the words flow without thinking about them.

You can also use a journal for the personal research we discussed in chapter eight. "What is my favorite color?" "Why do I believe this?" "What's my opinion about [insert issue here]?"

Journaling is sacred and effective, and you can discover so much about yourself that way. So schedule some time in your day for journaling and work through "Why can't I drive without having a panic attack?" See what comes up.

At the end of the day, write about how everything went. This way you can actually track your progress. "Yesterday was a little shaky, but I made it to work without any issues. Today, I stopped for coffee on the way to work, and that made it easier to drive once I had a coffee to fuel me and keep my mind distracted."

It's like scientific notes but for your life. Write about what worked, what didn't, what you'd like to see improve. Journaling is dreaming and dreaming is visualizing, therefore, you guessed it, you can use journaling to manifest healing for yourself and anything else you want in life.

The Walk/Run Method

You may be feeling overwhelmed at this point, but you don't have to run a marathon all the way through. Did you know that many runners choose a method called the walk/run method where they run for a while, then walk for a bit before running again? The same can work for you! Take a short trip for your first drive or stop for coffee on your way to work to break up the commute. Pausing to regroup and relax isn't failure. Nothing is failure. It's just another tool on your way to success.

Additionally, there are tools you can simply carry with you throughout the day to set you up for success wherever you go. Keeping lavender essential oil or an amethyst crystal in your purse will help with the energy around you and bring you calm without you having to focus on anything.

By doing one or all of these, you're setting your anxiety level to zero before you even turn the key in your car. Any anxiety that appears after that has a lot more building to do before it affects you than it would have if your anxiety meter was already at fifty percent when you started.

And once you get in the car, repeat your intention for the drive. Remind yourself that no matter what, you will have a safe and efficient drive. Take deep breaths, choose a soothing radio station if you like to listen to specific music that you know will help you feel calm or even excited – anything you want that isn't panic, and understand that if you need to pull over and take a break, that is totally okay.

These are only physical examples of how you can take control of your day and arrange your time so panic attacks are a non-issue for you. In chapter ten, I'll show you the most effective tools that, when paired with these, will make you into the superwoman you know you are meant to be. The one who never gives anxiety a second thought and drives wherever in the world she wants to go with whomever she chooses.

Rest Stop: Your Daily Planner

Let's plan your personal toolkit in your journal.

- When are you going to allow yourself mental breaks throughout the day?
- What space can you organize to set yourself up for less stress?
- What are your intentions for everything you have scheduled today?
- Is there a question you have for yourself that you'd like to answer with journaling?

Chapter Ten:

Find Your Driving Zen

You now understand how to go about your day without allowing anxiety to be an issue physically. Now we're going to cement everything you've learned so far so you can do anything you need to from now on.

Remember in chapter eight when we talked about feelings being your front line of experience with the world? In this chapter, I'm going to give you simple tools and practices that you can do regularly to retrain your brain and change the way your body reacts to the situations that triggered your anxiety before.

Affirmations

The first thing I recommend to anyone, because the options are absolutely limitless, is reciting affirmations. You already got a taste of my enthusiasm for this in chapter six. Affirmations are simply positive statements that you use to reprogram your subconscious beliefs. It's exactly what we did in the Coin Flip exercise and with changing your thoughts. Now that you realize what you were doing, you can use it.

In my motivational podcast, I take situations and make an affirmation out of them to help listeners conquer things like jealousy, anxiety, fear, you name it, but every episode starts with what I call the Big 3 daily affirmations.

I believe these affirmations work in any given situation, so even if you can't come up with your own, these three always have you covered. They are:

- "I overcome obstacles with renewed inner strength."
- "I am successful in all that I do."
- "Gratitude is my attitude."

Say them out loud and see how they feel. Do you believe yourself when you say them?

I believe these three phrases can get you through anything because they complement each other so well. One leads into the other to take you from the beginning of a challenge all the way through to the end. If you understand that you overcome obstacles and become stronger, then you realize that the obstacles are actually serving to help you level up in life like a character in a video game or the hero of a story. When you view obstacles as quests or missions that are leveling you up to face the next thing, it becomes more fun. And approaching things with a playful mindset keeps you calm. What if you thought driving was fun and treated it like a video game (obviously not an aggressive video game)? How would it be different for you?

Maybe you don't like video games, but the point remains the same. You are always growing and becoming something more than you were before. That's what leveling up is. It's building upon what you have to make something stronger.

Once you have that mindset about obstacles, they don't get you down so much because you can see the purpose in them a lot sooner than if you'd have to wait for hindsight. And through that understanding, you come to realize that you truly are always successful, because you learn that if you level up with every challenge you face, then those challenges are guiding you toward success.

You stop believing in coincidence and see the world for what it is: the reality you co-create around you.

This also helps when you feel like you've failed, which you never do. The idea of failure is just your brain trying to give you an excuse to stop. If you don't stop, you won't fail because you'll see the situation through to completion, and what is completion? Success!

Mixing this concept with your understanding of divine timing, you start to see that even when things don't turn out the way you'd hoped, it isn't because you failed, it's because the time wasn't right. You don't control divine timing, so how can it be your failure? It's simply that you are going to get something *better*, something that fits you perfectly. Don't feel disappointed – get excited!

You don't want to shove your puzzle piece into a space where it doesn't fit perfectly. You want to find that perfect space, the one that was always meant for only you, and if this opportunity wasn't the perfect fit, not only do you not want it anyway, but you now have two things to be happy about: a) you're getting something better than you expected that *will* be your perfect fit, and b) you didn't take up a space that is someone else's perfect fit. You've helped them by leaving it available for them to find. You're a good person.

Now all you have to do is check your divine timing, and keep an eye out for better opportunities.

That's where gratitude comes in. First, because you can be grateful for growing stronger and understanding that you get to dream bigger than you thought you deserved, and second because gratitude helps with the stress of waiting.

Finding three things to be grateful for every day or in every difficult situation will pull you out of panic and out of the nervousness of a challenge to give you a more objective point of view. You'll see there isn't anything for you to be worried about, and you'll be more in the moment.

Use these affirmations to get you started and I guarantee you'll be crafting your own affirmations in no time. Simply take your negative feeling, and rephrase it as a positive statement in the present tense. They can be as simple as, "Driving is safe." "My trips are always worry-free."

Using the present tense is important because it does a magical thing. It transforms you then and there. You're not saying, "My trips will be worry-free." When is "will?" How do you know when it's happened? Instead, claiming that your trips are already worry-free tells you that it's your truth from this moment on. You are no longer the woman you were a second ago. You've made a decision and changed completely. You are, as of now and forevermore, the fearless woman. You don't have to go back and you don't have to wait for anything else to fall into place. You've already succeeded. All you have to do now is live like that woman lives, because she is you, and your trips are perfect.

Have you ever heard someone say, "Oh, I don't get sick," and then you realize they really don't? That's because they believe it, and so it is.

Manifesting.

Affirmations are also a great way to introduce your mind to meditation and mindfulness.

Meditation

Let me debunk something for you: You don't have to have a clear mind to successfully meditate. I have been doing intuitive work my whole life and actively using my intuition to coach and help people for more than ten years, and never once have I meditated with a completely clear mind.

Some people can think about nothing, but I'm not one of them and if you have a tendency toward panic attacks, I'm guessing a clear mind sounds pretty foreign to you too.

Meditation isn't the act of thinking nothing. It's a way to bring your mind into the present and zoom out from life to see the bigger picture, or to find calm and relaxation. You can't do it wrong because it's going to happen in whatever way works best for you.

Many people use yoga, others use music, you can even use your affirmations and just repeat them for a few minutes. However you find your Zen is how you meditate. For me, writing is meditative. Journaling is a form of meditation. Knitting has been considered a form of meditation. Use one of these ideas or make up your own, but don't worry about comparing your connection to God/the Universe/Source with anyone else's. That's only going to stress you out even more.

I prefer to structure my whole life (no surprise since I'm a Taurus), so I do this with my Zen time as well. Every morning after breakfast, I sit at a bamboo shoe rack that I put a bunch of crystals and things on, and I practice my version of meditation. I go over my daily planner, checking my astrology and numerology for any divine timing I can use to set my intentions for the day, then say a prayer to claim those intentions out loud with God (co-creation). Finally, I cap it off with a daily oracle card spread, mostly for the fun of it and to get extra insight on how I can make the most of my day.

Oracle cards are awesome because they can guide you with specific questions. I use spreads that fall in line with the phases of the moon so they guide me with divine timing as an added benefit. They help me decide where I should direct my energy, bring clarity to things that I worry about in the future, and help me feel a sense of understanding in what's happening around me as

I wait for divine timing to align with my timing. One might even call that patience, or at least my definition of patience.

Once I have all that information, if I have any questions left, I'll meditate for about a minute or two, depending on how busy my brain feels that day.

Your Intuition

Meditating in the traditional sense gives you a unique opportunity to hear God for yourself. That's another thing they preached to me as a kid that never made sense until I did it on my own terms: having a personal relationship with God.

It seemed unattainable, but one thing I've learned in my years of doing readings and offering healing and coaching is that my real job is to teach people how to talk to God for themselves, because everyone is capable of it. You don't have to see auras or speak to the dead to practice your own spiritual gifts. Everyone is born with enough of a sixth sense to connect to the creative source. Whether you call Him God, the Universe, Source, or She, it still counts. The fact that you have a name for the Creator is proof that you've already started to form that relationship. These practices are teaching you how to control your life, but the ultimate way to understand your life with your divine timing is to have a connection with the energy that controls divine timing.

It doesn't have to come in the form of a booming voice in the clouds. I don't know a single person that hears God that way, but that's what most people are looking for.

No, it's usually in your gut instincts, in the alignments around you, in the random urges and thoughts that you just can't shake. I can assure you, your connection is already there. All you have to do is recognize it, and you'll be able to add that to your routine as well. Imagine never feeling anxious again because you understand the world around you from a divine perspective. Imagine asking a question and getting an answer, praying and actually getting a response.

Maybe you've had that happen a time or two, and now you realize what it was. Now you can make something with it. If you can't identify that experience for yourself yet, these tools will help you get there. Noticing the synchronicities around you as you'll do with your divine timing is noticing the divine working around you. Turns out you have experience with your personal connection with God after all.

That's why I add all of this into my daily routine. It's like flexing a muscle and keeping it in shape. The more I do it, the easier and clearer it becomes. And it never comes from a place of anger. It never leaves me feeling anything less than unique and absolutely loved and capable.

This morning prayer ritual sets the tone for the entire day and prepares me for anything. I know who I'm meeting, what I'm doing, when I'm doing it, and I can organize all of that in line with my personal divine timing.

Mindfulness

That's how I find my Zen as someone who enjoys control. Yes, my name is KristaLyn and I am a control freak. But just like the Coin Flip exercise in chapter six, if you flip control what do you get? Mindfulness.

Mindfulness, by my definition, is the act of using the information around me to live in the moment. I have no reason to worry about what comes next because it's already been scheduled. The same way God has a plan for my life, I have a plan for my day that aligns with His plan. If something random happens, I can rework that schedule, because I know my resources before I even start my day. I set intentions before everything. If a client calls asking for a last-minute session, I take thirty seconds, breathe, and decide how I'm going to be during that session, what that looks like, and if it's even a good idea or if it's something I should say no to.

Saying no is a spiritual act and an important part of manifesting an anxiety-free reality. It may stress you out to think about saying no, but that's only because you're worried about what might happen. "But, my darling, what if you fly?" What if that person you say no to learns your boundaries and learns by extension how to respect you in a kind way? You will have fewer and fewer things to say no to because people will understand you, and they won't put you in those situations to begin with. You'll have less to stress about because your tasks in a day will be manageable. You won't have to factor in a dreaded destination as part of the reason you're panicking on a drive. You'll be doing your research on who you are and what's important to you and living your life aligned with who you are.

Remember, you are intentional. Your personality, preferences, all those things are part of your divine timing, and if you choose to say no, you are living according to your divine timing just as much as when you choose to say yes. Don't worry about letting people down. You're simply saying, "I can't do this task justice the way you deserve and I think someone else would be better suited for it." It's not your puzzle piece space.

There is no shame in choosing to be yourself and sticking with your own priorities.

Your life is yours to live, your days are yours to fill with things that bring you joy and occasionally obstacles that make you stronger. You can know the difference by checking your divine timing and making your spiritual health a part of your daily routine, and none of it is selfish. Once you feel safe and cared for, you create space to help others.

Rest Stop: Build Your Ritual

Think about your style. What does a morning ritual look like for you? What tools help you feel more in control and calm? Perhaps it's listening to a motivational podcast or an audiobook on your drive to work. Maybe you like to have a quick morning yoga flow to get you started and center your energy. Whatever it is, you can design a daily routine that puts your mind in the present and prepares you for the day rather than slinging yourself into the day feeling unprepared and anxious. I've given you a few ideas for you to copy over to your journal below. Add to it and make it yours!

All you have to do is decide that you're going to do it and find a way to commit. How likely are you to stick to it? What will motivate you to do the things you know will help you?

Morning Ritual

Exercise/Meditation:

Intention:

Scheduled Me Time:

Daily Affirmation:

Three Things I'm Grateful For:

1.

2.

3.

To-do List:
Intention for each to-do:

Chapter Eleven:

Navigating the Road Ahead

When trying to conquer anxiety, most people come at it from an angle of...anxiety. They view the anxiety as some rare species of monster that has no known weakness and comes from some netherworld only to devour everything in its path, and they bow down to it.

And this is how they accept their reality from then on, allowing panic to take the wheel.

You do not have to be that girl.

That girl breaks down because she doesn't feel like she has any support from friends, loved ones, or someone who's been where she is and has come through it. She feels like she's in this alone and to tell people that she's suffering would be seen as weakness. So she hides it and lets it grow, unchecked into an even bigger monster.

Even if she picks herself up and tries to conquer her anxiety on her own, constantly getting in the car and trying again, the minute that anxiety crops up, she retreats. It gets too hard to face it over and over again without the best tools to overcome it. The anxiety controls the car, and so she fears the car and the anxiety.

So many people forget that consistency is a part of every process, not just manifesting but all things. How did you graduate from school? You showed up every day. Why? Because you had a routine and the incentive to stick with it.

Anyone who's ever successfully lost weight knows this. You show up every day, even though it can be hard, even when you don't feel like it, and eventually, you are an entirely new version of yourself who doesn't carry around that extra weight, physically *and* metaphorically.

How much does your anxiety weigh on you? Do you believe in yourself enough to show up? Without a reason why you're doing something, it's hard to stick with it and you begin to doubt that you were ever capable of it in the first place. But you've done hard things before. This is just a new hard thing and it's only hard for as long as it takes for you to adjust to it and overcome it – which you *can* do.

The world may tell you it's not possible. You will see relatable memes all over social media validating your anxiety, almost praising you for your suffering, but is suffering what you want to be praised for? Do you want to settle into your anxiety and wear it as a badge of honor, or do you want to wear a badge of courage and mental health and joy?

The people posting those memes on social media aren't your people. They're not the tribe you're searching for. They aren't ready to get back behind the wheel. Staying curled up with a laptop and making excuses about why they should continue to suffer instead of having to try or change appeals more to them, but not to you.

You wouldn't be here if you were like them. You need to surround yourself with people who keep pushing forward until they see results. Your tribe is full of people who know their worth and help you see your own. You can even be the one to start that tribe and show others the worth in them because you've found the worth in you.

The fearless woman takes the drive into her own hands rather than going into the situation unprepared over and over again, losing motivation after too many failures to count. Remember, it's only failure if you give up, if you stop. You don't stop because you know if you aren't happy, then it isn't over.

If you want to be the woman who gets behind the wheel and drives without fear of a panic attack, you know what to do. You've made it this far and this book is yours to keep. If you choose to, you can overcome this and nothing will stand in your way again.

You're going to have days when these thoughts pop up. Your brain is going to try to tell you to go back to the safe place where fear keeps you cooped up in your house while everyone else gets to have adventures. I'm not saying it's going to be the easiest thing you've ever done, but what I do believe for you with my whole heart is that it will be the best thing you've ever done, and it will take you beyond driving, beyond anxiety, beyond what you thought the world was before you read this book.

You now have access to the secret behind life and reality. You have nothing to fear from this moment on. It'll be a daily practice remembering that, but the tools are all here for you to reference whenever you need them. You can use exactly what this book tells you to do and it will work, or you can adapt these tools and techniques to suit your own style and that's totally fine too.

The only thing I hope you don't do is nothing. Now that you understand that you create the world around you, that you can change your reality to make it anything you dream of (remember the theta brain wave is the one we use to dream, daydream, and be creative), I hope you claim it and thrive in that co-creative process. I hope you chase your dreams, take adventures, make memories, help people, and go through life compiling the most epic stories that no social media feed could hope to accurately capture.

You are magic. Not the Halloween costume, hocus-pocus kind of magic, but the real kind that we all have and forget to use.

Don't let anyone tell you can't do something. You control your life and they control theirs, but they have no say in how you choose to live. They only project their fears onto you so they will feel validated. Love them. Bless them in their process. But you don't need excuses.

There are plenty of resources out there selling the excuse that anxiety is something you just have to live with. There are even articles that explain how to overcome it, but none of them will connect with you on a level that makes sense if you don't become the fearless woman now.

Rest Stop: Detours

What obstacles do you think you might face moving forward? Write them down in your journal along with your plan to conquer them!

Potential Detours:

How I will navigate them:

Chapter Twelve:

Life Is Your Highway

know you still have questions, and the road ahead may still feel a bit foggy, but you already know that the journey is what you decide it will be. You can set your intentions for this process the same way you would for a drive or any other life event that comes your way. You are not alone, whether mentally, physically, or spiritually. The power to find the purpose behind your accident and make use of the lessons it taught you so that life doesn't have to feel so out of control is just a daily decision away.

You can use these journal pages and release your anxieties to the Universe. They're not yours anymore.

All you have to do now is decide to show up for yourself and commit to making a habit of it. Change the thoughts that scare you. Teach your mind to embrace the world in all its beautiful unpredictability. Use your resources to prepare for everything you can possibly see coming with divine timing on your side, and handle surprises with a playful attitude instead of fear. If you aren't happy, it isn't over.

You don't need anyone to give you permission to heal or to make these changes for yourself. You can find more motivation in yourself and the strengths you were born with than any social media hashtag can conjure up for you, and you can find people who understand you and support you as you grow through this process into the fearless woman.

I realize this is all well and good to say, but you have everything you need to start doing it.

The Driven Fearless Woman

- Knows that she doesn't have to spend the rest of her life battling anxiety.
- Wants to feel safe, calm, and confident so she can drive with the wind in her hair.
- Understands how to plan for unexpected situations to avoid any more accidents.

- Knows what triggers her panic attacks and that they can be prevented on both physical and on emotional levels.
- Knows she has the tools to navigate any obstacles if she chooses to use them.

You went through something hard, and every road to recovery is a unique experience, but you don't have to limit yourself to the belief that panic attacks are some incurable disease. You can get behind the wheel and drive safely to any destination you choose, because you know how to handle even the unexpected, and you understand the world on a deeper level than most people who don't have to suffer through anxiety do.

Now you have everything you need to not only conquer your panic attacks, but take control of your entire life and live it consciously and with joy. You may still get a shiver when you think about driving, but you don't have to do it all at once as long as you decide that you *will* do it, follow through, and stick to it.

Acknowledgments

Where do I even begin with the amount of gratitude I feel in this moment, the culmination of everything I've done in my life so far? First and always, I thank God for all the good things, but especially the difficult things that have carved and shaped me into the person He always intended for me to become. Also, my endless gratitude to Dr. Scott who took my life into his hands and performed a miracle on the operating table, and without whom I probably would not be here today.

Speaking of miracles and making things possible, I am overjoyed to have worked with the incredible editors, Mehrina and Moriah, and the others at the Author Incubator, Ramses and Cheyenne. Thank you for making space for my success and for teaching me what it feels like to do it for myself and for others. You are all an inspiration to me and I am so blessed to have worked with you!

Angela Lauria, you already know this, but you are a rock star and I could not have achieved this dream as quickly and enjoyably without you. What an incredible adventure this has been and continues to be! Thank you for putting your faith in people like me and showing us how to take a message and mold it into a platform. My mind is blown.

Thank you to David Hancock and the Morgan James Publishing team for helping me bring this book to print.

Unlimited and unconditional love to my parents who have gone through so much with me and for me in so many ways, and who raised me to be strong, confident, and capable of anything I set my mind to. I will spend the rest of my life thanking you, and I will always use Vetovich as my pen name because I want people to know where I come from and that I am so proud to be your daughter.

To Shaun and Kristy, remember what you said at your Eagle ceremony? Same.

To Betty, who introduced me to a world of possibilities with energy and showed me where to find my center, and Sherry, who saw this whole thing coming ten years ago.

Thank you both for giving me the confidence to trust this crazy life and dive in.

To Laura, who has always accepted me no matter what kind of crazy I present to her, and my incredible Theta group who have shown me what the coveted "tribe" really feels like. Thank you all for showing me that true friendship really does accept you for who you are. Most of all to Dan, the best friend and husband I could have dreamed of. You are my constant, daily reminder that magic is real purely because you exist in my life.

And a very special place in this list of blessings goes to Diane. I know you're seeing this and I know you're not at all surprised. You always knew this would happen and you never doubted. You trusted me and became my greatest, wisest teacher, and I will never ever forget how you shaped me.

Finally, but not least of all, to you, the reader. The one who found enough value in the contents of this book to read even the Acknowledgments. I see you and I appreciate you. Thank you for following me all the way here. I hope I get to meet you someday so I can thank you in person! May these tools serve you in the highest and best way to lead you to a life a grace, ease, and joy!

Excerpt from

Strayed
KristaLyn's Latest Fiction Novella

Chapter 1

Well, it's happened again. I'm dead.

The bloodied sand of the colosseum shivers out of focus as my soul shakes off its physical limitations in favor of a higher plane of existence. Instead of centurions and weeping family, snowy-white noise and quiet now surround me.

They came for me at dawn. I can still hear my mother's sobs. I was only twelve.

I blink the memories away just as a man bends and pulls into view before me, then straightens with a blithe sort of smile. "Welcome back." He checks an invisible list somewhere behind his eyelids for my name. "Welcome back, Agnes." He wears glasses I know he doesn't need, and behind them, his unearthly blue eyes trace my face, looking for signs of stress.

And it comes back to me like the snap of fingers. An Advokat. Here to help me adjust to the trauma of crossing over from life to death.

Suddenly, I wonder how he sees *me*. Do I have blue eyes now? In life, they were brown, but here, in death, I've always imagined others see them as crystal blue. I guess it would depend on how much they like me. Appearance is entirely based on impression here. We see what we feel. Feelings are real, vision an illusion.

And this Advokat must be new, I realize a moment later. If he'd been here for any length of time, he wouldn't be using the sappy voice they put on for the newer souls—the ones who don't understand how it works.

I hold the record for most reincarnations in a single millennium. I've lost count of how many of these interviews I've had to sit through. I'm sure I know this process better than he does.

I've even had his job before, mastered it long ago.

I skim him, searching the endless trove of memories, trying to break through the fog of earthly business still clouding my mind. I don't remember him. And I can see that he doesn't know me.

He's definitely new, which means he'll play the interview by the book. I groan.

The Advokat reaches out as if to comfort me, as if my groan were one of anxiety and not disdain. "Try not to panic."

I resist the urge to roll my eyes and flatten my gaze at him instead. I understand it's his job to help me recover from the shock of death, but honestly, I'm fine. So I died–so what? There are many things worse than death, and one of them, if anyone ever bothered to ask me, is living. It actually thrills me to be back here–and I don't need an Advokat to counsel me through the transition.

Also, I'm in a bit of a hurry. I have important business to attend to, even higher vibrations to achieve. I'm so close now, and he's the only thing standing in my way.

I tap my foot and glance around for someone–anyone who might recognize me and give me an opportunity to walk away from this unnecessary formality.

"Everything will make sense soon." The Advokat's voice echoes through the white expanse around us. Clearly, all other souls are keeping their distance to allow me to transition without any added shock. Or–I narrow my eyes at the Advokat—he's followed protocol by requesting they give us space.

And do we ever have it. As far as the eye can see, there's nothing but static white. But I smile and my shoulders relax because this is my true home—just the way I remember it.

The Advokat leans into my line of sight. "Do you know your name?" My smile drops.

In life, my name was Agnes, just as he said before—in this *life, anyway.*

I have had so many lives, so many names, but of them all, just one feels like home. When it comes, my voice sounds like a lost, cherished memory. "Anaya." My first word after death. The truest word I know.

The Advokat smiles and nods. He doesn't take any notes or write anything down, and I know about that too. The answers appear in his mind, ready when he needs them, downloaded into his head from the source of all truth on the highest plane of vibration that exists: El Olam, our master and creator. He sits so high none of us can reach him, above laws and structure. The world is as he makes it, and we are simply stewards of his creation, here to serve.

And today, I'll go one step further down the path as a defender of creation. I'll become a Firn, a spirit guide to humans.

The Advokat, who annoys me more and more by the moment, interrupts my thoughts with yet another question. "Good. And do you know where you are?"

Where I am? Well, it's a much better place than where I was.

I was in Rome, in the fourth century. I rejected a boy, and he sold me out as a Christian. It took the soldiers forever to kill me–first with shame, then with flames. But all I gave them was a blank stare through the numbness. They couldn't shame me. I wouldn't burn when they strung me to the stake and lit the fire–even the flames knew not to touch me. But the Roman officer's sword through my throat did the trick in the end. I was gone before I felt anything. So I guess the joke's on them. There was darkness, then a burst of light–

And now I'm home, where none of that matters anymore. I'm free here because no one can shame or kill the dead. I'll be safe as long as I stay.

"This is Lemayle," I say quietly. "The afterlife. The real world." And I have no intention of ever living again.

He rocks back and grins. "Wonderful!" Then his face stiffens. He swallows and his eyes shake as he looks me over for a second time, now scanning for any truths beneath the surface, anything I'm hiding from him. If souls could sweat, he'd be a mess as he prepares for the most important question of the interview.

My answers from here on out will decide my final destination.

"All right." He clears his throat. He doesn't have to. It's the nerves. I will become his enemy if I answer poorly, but he has to remain objective. He's a professional, after all, and he doesn't yet know whose side I'm on—what changes this most recent lifetime might have made in me.

I was martyred, and not all martyrs come back home the way they should. Martyrs go into life as warriors for El Olam's cause but don't always return feeling it justified their suffering. Some turn against him and defect to the one who seeks to depose him.

And me? How do *I* feel about the suffering I was put through? Have I changed my mind about who to serve? And how dangerous does that make me to the fragile balance of the world? That's what the Advokat needs to find out.

"Do the names El Olam and Narn mean anything to you?"

Good and evil—that's what they mean. Free will and slavery. But which is which? Is El Olam good … or is he evil? Are Narn's plans for less service to humans and more dominion over them more appealing?

Are they justified? No souls *choose* evil. They simply choose what they believe is right.

I hide my laugh with a cough at the tension in the Advokat's hunched shoulders. If he's new—and he wants to stay—he'll need a stiffer spine than he's got now. I might as well be the one to give it to him.

I level my gaze at him, eyes wide open to appear just a little less threatening. "Yes. I know them."

He nods, more rigidly this time, and rubs the back of his neck as he braces for my response to his final question.

"And ... your allegiance?"

I stare at him for a long moment, watching the anxiety build behind his bright blue eyes. He doesn't want any trouble, but his other hand twitches at his side, ready to summon the support of a slightly higher power—just in case I came back tainted. Just in case I've decided I hate the way the world works ... and want to serve the one trying to turn it upside down.

"Oh, calm down," I finally chide him. This has gone on long enough to bore me. I have business to attend to, and honestly, after fifty lifetimes, a soul should be able to just skip this process. "I chose El Olam lifetimes ago. I'm bound to be a Firn. This was my last run."

His whole-body wilts as the tension releases. Had I said Narn, the Advokat and I would have had a few issues. It would have meant I was a soul with eyes toward flipping the script, turning the world upside down—forcing humans to do as we say and ruling over them as gods.

He'd have had to immediately summon one of Lemayle's second-highest authorities—a Malekh, one of

El Olam's archangels who exist exclusively in Lemayle, too good to need lifetimes of growth–to deal with me. And it wouldn't have been pleasant. The Malekh don't like jokes. Most of them, anyway.

"Well, that is a relief." The Advokat's hand slides from the back of his neck to clutch his chest, steadying the phantom sensation of a palpitating heart.

And I grin, even though I shouldn't. But what's the fun in seniority if you can't mess with the rookies?

"We need as many Firns as we can get," he admits, "events accelerating as they are." I perk up at that. *Accelerating events* is much more my speed–though it gives me less time to meet the final criteria for joining the Firns' ranks. "The humans need all the protection we can give them," he finishes.

I couldn't agree more. And that's where I come in–where all the Firns stand and serve El Olam. Without Firns to guide humans and protect them from temptation and harm, Narn *would* flip the script. And humans would walk right into their own slavery. But El Olam won't allow it. So neither will I.

I'm *so close* now. Just one step left, and if I impress the Malekh and El Olam enough in my next job as a soul collector, then I'll become a Firn, and one day, I'll become even more than that. If I perform well enough, I'll be chosen as the Firn who oversees El Olam's Plan to defeat Narn once and for all. One of us has to do it, so it might as well be me. And I won't stop until I see it happen.

Meanwhile, the Advokat extends his hand to me. "Best of luck to you. I hope you make the cut."

I glance at his hand and back up to him. So he really *hasn't* heard of me, then. I may not be a Firn yet, but I *have* made a name for myself as the one to watch for earning the coveted position in El Olam's Plan.

Well, if he hasn't heard of me yet, he will soon enough.

"Thanks." With a smirk, I grip his hand and shake it firmly enough to knock him off balance. "But I really don't need luck."

Thank You!

want to thank you – not only for reading my book but for standing up for yourself and for the joyful quality of life you deserve. I know you've already dealt with so much stress and maybe even criticism from people who don't understand what you're going through, but you never gave up on yourself, and that is incredible!

It is my sincere wish that upon finishing this book, you maintain that momentum and continue to become the unstoppable force you are meant to be.

As a way to say thank you for standing up for yourself and to help you with that journey, I'd love to offer you a safe and encouraging support system to guide you through your process without leaving space for anxiety to stop you. Follow me on Instagram @AuthorKristaLyn and I will provide you with daily inspiration and encouragement to guide you through this incredible process!

If you are interested in more holistic and spiritual methods to help conquer fear and anxiety, reach out to me at www.KristaLynAVetovich.com/lets-talk and we'll decide together if we're a good fit for your event or speaking engagements!

About the Author

KristaLyn is an internationally best-selling, certified holistic practitioner and intuitive coach who helps people attract the lives they want to live with the one thing they can't control: divine timing.

Graduating from Susquehanna University, KristaLyn knows what to do with a BA in English. She has published nearly ten books in both fiction and nonfiction, all with motivational themes of being your own hero and serving the world through your unique talents and gifts, which she knows everyone was born with.

For her thirteenth birthday, KristaLyn's mother took her on her first of many mission trips, introducing her to how a single person can make a large impact on the world, one fellow human being at a time. Thanks to this, KristaLyn has spent more than a decade serving others through coaching and holistic therapies. She is certified in life, spiritual, and health coaching, various holistic modalities including Reiki Master/Teacher, Crystal Healing, Advanced IET, and Advanced ThetaHealing®, with additional certifications in Hellenistic Astrology and Chirology.

A paragon of the millennial generation, KristaLyn entertained a variety of jobs ranging from amusement park showgirl, Group Mission Trips' Week of Hope Program Coordinator, and Disney World Cast Member as she pursued her dreams of sharing her message with the world.

KristaLyn lives in a treehouse in Elysburg, Pennsylvania with her husband and corgi, Jack, and cooperates with her family to help revitalize the Coal Region of Pennsylvania to a new, sustainable glory.

Website: www.KristaLynAVetovich.com
Email: info@KristaLynAVetovich.com
Social Media Handle: @AuthorKristaLyn

9 781642 798166